ADVANCE PRAISE

"As someone who is now free of atrial fibrillation and has taken on a mission to help people with AFib regain their lives and freedom, I found Jim's memoir authentic and inspiring. It chronicles how he built and sold a substantial training business while simultaneously in the throes of AFib, which is frightening and insidious. His entrepreneurial journey while surviving AFib provides optimism and hope for others living with this life-altering condition."

—MELLANIE TRUE HILLS, Survivor, heart health expert, motivational speaker, patient advocate, and founder of StopAfib.org

"Jim Kaveney's accomplishments as a businessman and entrepreneur—as detailed in *Unlimited Heart*—are impressive. I am inspired by his journey and am certain that Jim's next chapter in helping people with AFib navigate the physical, mental, and emotional complexities of this disease will fill a major gap in the AFib patient community and change lives. I look forward to watching Jim build his next business, Unlimited Heart Health & Wellness, as he offers lessons from his own experiences."

—GREG ROBITAILLE, Water Street Healthcare Partners

"A brave and honest personal journey of a modern miracle, Jim Kaveney's *Unlimited Heart* is heartfelt and gritty. Born into the great generation of hard-working families, Jim faces extraordinary challenges as he seeks true north. While navigating the evil disease of AFib, we gain insight into the power of love, humor, medicine, and support of family, colleagues, and friends. A fast-paced, compelling story that is a must-read for those with or without a master plan for life."

—LYNNE MURPHY, Pharmaceutical and biotech executive

"Both a universal and unique tale all at once, *Unlimited Heart* offers the reader the true gift of a deeply personal and vulnerable journey exemplifying the American Dream but wrapped in a package of triumph over unexpected and life-threatening health troubles. Kaveney's recounting of his childhood is so vivid, the reader can't help but see the entire backdrop where he learned his indomitable 'Kaveney Work Ethic'—a trait that would eventually both build his company and save his life. This brave telling allows the readers to feel exactly what Kaveney feels in his heart, both physically and metaphorically, and to ride the ups and downs with him, feeling every low and celebrating every win. Ultimately, it's Kaveney's heart, opened wide, leading the reader through this memoir, business tome, and love story."

—**AMY LABELLE,** Founder and winemaker at LaBelle Winery, attorney, *WSJ* bestselling author, entrepreneur, professional speaker, and coach

"In this gripping memoir, Jim bares his soul as he recounts the harrowing yet ultimately triumphant saga of his battle with a rare heart condition. As a devoted father, every heartbeat carries the weight of his family's love and his own unyielding determination combined with the 'Kaveney Work Ethic.' Jim invites you into the inner sanctum of his heart—both metaphorically and physically—revealing the raw emotions, the agonizing setbacks, and the miraculous moments from his formative years as a young man through his life-changing experience as a collegiate rower that defined his extraordinary journey. A testament to the power of the human spirit and the resilience of the human heart, *Unlimited Heart* is a stirring reminder that even in our darkest hours, the bonds of love and determination can light the way."

—**ADRIAN SPRACKLEN,** Director of Rowing, Mercyhurst University, Olympic rowing coach, 3x NCAA Champion, national team rower, and USA medical staff

"*Unlimited Heart* educated me on Jim's story, his dreams, his fears, and his loves. His bow tie tells his colleagues he has a unique style. His story tells readers how full a life he leads. And his heart tells everyone how impactful he is and continues to be. To say this book mesmerized me fails to describe the scale of emotions while reading. From the heights of humor to the depths of sadness in a matter of sentences, *Unlimited Heart* proves nothing short of a rapt reading experience."

—**MICHAEL HILLAN,** Business owner, pharmaceutical executive, author, and coach

Unlimited Heart

Unlimited Heart

How to Transform Your Pain into Purpose

JIM KAVENEY

IDEAPRESS
PUBLISHING

WASHINGTON, DC

IDEAPRESS
PUBLISHING

Ideapress Publishing | www.ideapresspublishing.com

All trademarks are the property of their respective companies.

Cover Design: Faceout Studio, Spencer Fuller
Illustrations: David Grillo
Interior Design: Jessica Angerstein

Cataloging-in-Publication Data is on file with the Library of Congress.

Hardcover ISBN: 978-1-64687-172-8

Special Sales
Ideapress Books are available at a special discount for bulk purchases for sales promotions and premiums, or for use in corporate training programs. Special editions, including personalized covers, a custom foreword, corporate imprints, and bonus content, are also available.

1 2 3 4 5 6 7 8 9 10

Contents

Part three

For Team K

My love for you can be found in my heart "section"

... And I You

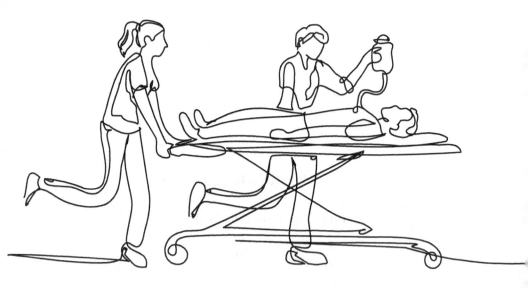

Prologue

Prologue

Norman Rockwell painting. It's really the only way to describe that night. A perfect night. It was a few days before Christmas, and the lights on the tree were glistening, and the house was glowing. The fireplace was crackling, keeping the cold New Hampshire wind from seeping into the family room. The picture-perfect scene was topped off by our family of four—plus our fourteen-year-old dog, Moxie—all snuggled around for movie night.

On such an occasion, there was only one obvious choice for what movie we picked.

Venom.

A traditional holiday classic in the Kaveney household. When you have two boys under the age of ten, every Marvel movie becomes an instant "classic." For them, *Venom* was the perfect choice for the perfect pre-Christmas movie night.

It wasn't long before my wife felt the stark contrast between the warmth of the Christmas lights and the cold plot of *Venom*. The parasitic, villain-centered film did not register highly on her holiday-spirit metric. Crazy, right? She and Moxie ducked out of the family room seeking the Christmas spirit elsewhere.

Spreading out and snuggling on the couch with my boys was the best. We made a dad sandwich, with one kid on the left, the other on the right, and my overjoyed self snuggled in the middle. We were warm and cozy, and the movie (for them) was perfect.

I was hit with the jolly gratitude of the Ghost of Christmas Present.

I was my kids' superhero.

I felt invincible.

I felt my heart grow bigger than the Grinch's.

I felt . . . my heart.

Literally.

My heart began to pulse at a pace that was way too aggressive for the moment. Take the most post-marathon, pre-first-kiss, public-speaking, night-before-a-wedding, heart-racing thing imaginable. Now, apply that feeling to simply lying on the couch doing nothing—a resting state.

I thought, *I am OK. I will be OK. It's an anomaly. This is not supposed to happen. Just a fluke. I'll take a few deep breaths, calm myself down, and return to my preferred superhero state.* As I took the first deep breath, I looked to my boys. The combination of the fireplace and cozy blankets had forced them to the edges of the couch to escape the heat. I shifted my focus back to the movie, hoping it would distract me from the panic wrestling to creep in.

But my attempts to breathe calmly and quietly weren't working. My heart was not slowing down. This was not a part of any Norman Rockwell painting I'd ever seen. *Shit.*

My thoughts were treading the waters of the darkness of the movie, the panic over my racing heart, the warmth of the too-warm fireplace, and the diatribe in the back of my mind saying: *Just stay calm.*

But my vision was blurring.

And my head was spinning.

And my heart would just not slow down.

And my spirit guide for all of this was Spider-Man's nemesis of all people.

And . . . the chaos *and fear* started to win.

I needed serious help.

I looked again at my boys, but they were deep into the movie. Why wouldn't they be? I hadn't made a peep. The screams of *danger* were all relegated to my mind and my heart. For all they knew, dear ole Dad was just fine, enjoying the movie just as much as they were, caught up in the drama that was *Venom*.

They had no idea what I was facing—what we as a family were about to face. Wanting to protect them and their enjoyment for even a few more minutes, I looked to the kitchen, to my wife.

Just stay calm.

Heart pulsing even higher and erratic, I called out softly.

"Lisa."

I could see her from my position on the couch, looking at the calendar on the kitchen wall. She didn't respond. The television's surround sound was doing its job and engulfed any whisper. My vision grew darker. My heart was completely out of control.

It was racing. Racing. *Racing*. Every fiber of my being was now on high alert. It felt like my heart was going to explode. I couldn't keep it inside any longer. I started to cry out and scream for Lisa because . . .

I was dying.

It had to be what dying felt like.

This was it.

Just stay calm.

The kids' attention shifted to me. Obviously scared, they joined in the screaming.

"LISA!"

"MOM!"

I stood and tried to walk to the kitchen, but that only made it worse. Lisa finally realized something was not right. I made it to the hutch under the television. My six-foot-six-inch frame crumbled under the absolute chaos inside me. That chaos was now echoed by the flurry of hands around me.

Lisa somehow managed to get me back to the couch. Tense, arched back, head nearly going through the wall while my heart and mind were synchronized in bringing me down. The fear was almost as all-consuming as the inability of my heart to slow its beat. Lisa was on the phone with 911 and shoved practically a whole bottle of aspirin into my mouth.

"Chew and swallow, chew and swallow," she said.

My boys were now upstairs, away from the scene, but they were looking down at me from the second floor. I couldn't even begin to imagine what was going through their minds. I could barely reconcile what was going on in my own mind.

The paramedics arrived and cut through my clothes, attaching all sorts of wires and working feverishly to reverse the course that my heart seemed set on. They quickly confirmed exactly what I knew: my heart was beating off-the-charts fast, with a resting heart rate of 240 beats per minute, four times my usual.

Not good.

Not good *at all*.

I was weak, panicking, and felt entirely out of control. Rockwell would not paint this scene. I can't imagine anyone in their right mind who would paint it. It was, factually, a shit show.

The crackling warmth of the fireplace was gone, replaced by the cold December winds as the paramedics rolled me out of the house and into the ambulance. My kids rushed to get to me, but my neighbor Lindsey was somehow on the scene and gently held them back. They called out to say they loved me. I was still their superhero. It was the only crack of light in the otherwise suffocating darkness that had taken over our perfect night.

Strapped in tight, ears roaring with the pounding of my heart and the screams of the siren, the doors of the ambulance shut behind me.

Part
one

CHAPTER 1

1, 2, 9 Rule Story

Not one, not two, not three, hell, not even four, five, six, seven, or eight, but nine kids in my family. To say that was a lot is the understatement of the century. We all had our place in the family. We took our given birth order and ran with it.

As the youngest, I assumed the responsibility of just telling people who looked at me with shock and awe on their faces that, "Yeah, we're Irish Catholic," which, in all honesty, was a bit of a stretch. Technically speaking, we are equally of German ancestry, but that's neither here nor there. Being *Irish* Catholic seemed to tell the story better, and everyone immediately "got it."

For my mother, each of her nine children was a blessing from God; for my father, each of his nine children represented a bottle of Jameson. A lot of people live by the rule that there is no such thing as "just one drink." When you go out, if you have one drink, it will invariably lead to two drinks, and by the end of the night, you somehow find yourself putting back your ninth. This rule was executed flawlessly by my parents, except instead of drinks, it manifested with the number of children, and because I am the ninth, I'm happy they kept going.

Somewhere between these polar opposites of Jesus and Jameson lay the truth of how we all came to exist. And I liked it that way. A story that blended gratitude for the miracle of life and a more intense version of the miracle at the wedding of Cana, but this time Jesus turned water into whiskey, not wine.

I grew up in the city of Erie, Pennsylvania, where there was a Catholic church every few miles and what seemed like unlimited bars feeding the confessionals prior to Sunday service. A true blue-collar, working, middle-class town filled with hard-working people.

I never considered my parents "blue collar." My dad was one of those men who had the same job at the same place for his entire career: IBM for thirty years. My mom was a schoolteacher and held many other odds-and-ends jobs to help cover costs, from selling newspaper subscriptions, selling windows, or delivering the *PennySaver* weekly paper—making some extra "pin" money, as she would say. My parents ensured that we always had what we *needed* because they could not afford what we *wanted*. I grew up not knowing any difference to the way things were.

My mom was one of six kids in another good-sized Irish/German Catholic family. My mother was born at the beginning of the Great Depression; her father was a prominent businessman in town and her mother managed the affairs of the house and kids. They were socialites, born and raised in the upper middle–class part of town.

My dad was the youngest of three, another Irish/German Catholic family (believe it or not, the Catholics really like to stick together). His father worked in the steel mills, and his mom tended to the kids and worked in a local department store. They were lower-middle class and truly lived on the *other side* of the tracks. My parents had the quintessential "upstairs-downstairs" kind of story.

But the thing about class . . . it doesn't matter how much money a family has. Tragedy can still sniff you out.

At the young age of fourteen, my mother and her siblings were orphaned and left to fend for themselves. Both of her parents died at the age of thirty-nine. It was a tragic story that remained very *hush-hush* for a long time in my family. The details of my mother's life could be a book unto itself. My grandmother was killed in New Mexico while running away with another man, and my grandfather committed suicide while in prison for issues related to his business. The newspapers glossed it over, and generational trauma sealed that gloss. My mother and her siblings had to grow up too quickly. There was to be no support for them. The scandal and shame left them on their own.

My father dealt with the loss of his own father just two days after he turned twenty-one. The story behind my paternal grandfather is murky at best and traumatic at worst. He was very hard on my dad—physically and emotionally—but to what extent, the details were never shared.

The early years of both my parents' lives were riddled with adversity and challenges. But they rolled with the punches because there was no other option. Nobody really likes the phrase "pick yourself up by the bootstraps" anymore, but this is exactly what my parents had to do.

The trickle-down effect of their childhoods and survival-mode methods made its way into our home and passed to all of us kids.

We called it the *Kaveney Work Ethic*.

If one of us wanted something, we had to work for it. Plain and simple. Set goals, establish a system to get there, and grind till achieved. There was no formal instruction. We just worked. If we were too young to make our own money, we worked in other ways to offset the cost of living. The goal wasn't to collect *things*, it was to put food on the table, some clothes on our backs, and have at least a little bit of family fun.

Having nine kids sounds crazy, even to someone who grew up with it, but my parents did not take the responsibility lightly. They never accepted handouts. They worked as many hours as needed to provide for each of us. They had their personal demons. Who doesn't? But they did what they could when they could to make our lives run smoothly.

There are nine different versions of how their personal struggles influenced us kids. This one is just mine.

Through my older siblings' eyes, I was born with a silver spoon in my mouth. The older eight paved the way for my "yellow-brick-road" lifestyle through the sacrifices they made with my parents. I would hear stories about how a night out on the town for them was a bag of McDonald's cheeseburgers and my dad's homemade milkshakes. I, on the other hand, would get treated to surf and turf on a regular basis.

That's . . . technically . . . only partially . . . true. But, when you do the math, the more kids who grew up and left the house, the more "disposable" income the family had for those of us still living together. Less mouths to feed naturally led to more "pin" money . . . and a shrimp cocktail or two. It was nice, but it was no silver spoon.

My parents believed in the value of education, and they made sure that we got the absolute best they could provide, which of course meant Catholic schooling for all nine of us. Faith and education helped my mother overcome the trauma of being orphaned at such a young age, and she and my dad knew they would do the same for all of us—minus the being orphaned part.

Even though my childhood home was across the street from a public school, my parents made us walk the few blocks to St. Andrew's. They would let us play our days away in the playground across the street, but our minds, faith, morals, and handwriting would be shaped elsewhere. Just because one school was closer did not mean it was the right fit for everyone. They were convinced that a few extra blocks would make a world of difference in our lives.

My oldest sister—JoAnne—was fourteen when I was born. We were all roughly two years apart with one almost set of Irish twins—they missed this feat by seventeen days. Apparently, that third bottle of Jameson kept my dad out of the game for a few days. Nine kids spanning fourteen years meant a continued flow of kids through grade school, high school, and college at any given time . . . and a continued flow of money out the door and into the pockets of school administration.

When my dad was forced into retirement from IBM at the age of sixty, his final salary was $37,500. I was a senior in high school with four years of college ahead of me. My mom ended up teaching until she was seventy-two, and her final salary was not much more than my dad's. My parents could never be accused of rolling in the cash. So how did they pay for all that schooling?

Coupons!

. . . and a healthy dose of pride.

That's how my family managed this feat. I remember being at the grocery store and my mom handing me a coupon for buy-one-get-one-free Banquet chicken. The only problem was that there was a limit of one per family, which just would not do for the size of my family. She separated me and two of my sisters into separate checkout lines so that we could each count as a "family" and get two boxes of frozen chicken for $2.50.

My mother.

She could stretch a dollar like no one else and, more importantly for her, this allowed her to steer clear of having to accept a handout from anyone.

We were *working* poor. Life is about choices, and she taught us to take personal responsibility, work hard, and have faith. She was full of grit. She was forced into survival mode too early in life. She overcame most of the odds stacked against her. And she made damn sure to never slip in her mind-set of self-determination. Her heart was set on living life a certain way. And we did exactly as she taught us.

Coupons were good for food, but the money saved wasn't exactly enough to get nine kids through private education.

But child labor was.

If my five brothers and I agreed to work as altar servers at our parish, the school would provide discounted tuition. For every additional sibling in attendance, the price per child went down. Thankfully, my parents kept a steady flow of children enrolled to keep the discount coming.

To accommodate this deal, we were at church for what felt like every single day of my existence. Monday through Saturday Mass was held at 5:30 and 6:30 in the morning. It's not hard to imagine why we considered ourselves in the throes of child labor at such *ungodly* hours of the morning. Sunday was our literal heaven on earth since Masses didn't start until 8:00 a.m. Sleeping in on Sunday mornings was the highlight of the week.

For my parents, the grueling back-and-forth journey between church, home, and school wasn't grueling at all—or, at least, not that they ever let on. For them, the benefits of church paying for school went hand in hand, as both our minds and our hearts received top-tier education.

When I was in kindergarten, my parents had five kids in grade school, two in high school, and two in college. My parents did not have a formal system to maintain the cashflow; they just stuck to the habits that would get us all through it. My mom did not formally begin working until I could safely walk to school without a parent.

After it was all said and done, my parents found a way to pay for 144 collective years of Catholic education.

Let me repeat myself in case that did not sink in.

One hundred forty-four collective *years* of private education.

Call it stubbornness. Call it pride. Call it insane. Call it whatever you want. At the end of the day, my parents ensured that we *always* got what we needed. Even if it wasn't what we wanted at the time. Even if the strapped cash of the week led to more coupons clipped and more altars served. There remained constant conviction in their determination to put us all through this kind of education system, and they made sure to achieve it.

CHAPTER 2

Shadow of Light

Every child should be shielded from adult problems and hold onto their innocence, playfulness, and curiosity. For all intents and purposes, my early childhood was like that.

Straightforward.

Black and white.

My greatest worry was only what activity or toy was going to be played with next. My parents made sure I was clean, clothed, fed, and loved. Even with eight older siblings, there always seemed to be enough to go around. I truly didn't know it could be any different. For as much love as was given, I would work to return it even more. Even though I was the baby, I was *everyone's* favorite . . . or so they always said.

The picture I've painted of my family story is every bit true, but beyond the black-and-white, true-grit American narrative, there was not only gray but also a whole lot of . . . color.

I can remember innocently riding with my dad in our station wagon, with no seatbelt, sitting on top of a case of long-neck Budweiser, drinking an orange pop that the beer distributor gave to me. I can't remember the frequency of those trips, but they were often.

Those trips to the store were usually followed by a Kaveney family gathering. We had a very social family with a lot of aunts, uncles, and cousins. Always hanging out, eating, and drinking. This was all fun and games to be around as a young kid. So much energy. So much life. So much to observe.

But when the extended family wasn't around, the drinking didn't stop for my dad. My mom wasn't a teetotaler—she liked her whiskey highballs—but she saw the devastation alcohol brought to her own mom, dad, and siblings and limited her consumption. With nine kids, there was clearly no time for a mother-sized hangover.

My father took the . . . opposite . . . approach to day-to-day coping mechanisms. Over the years, he became more and more reclusive. The more reclusive he became, the more strain was put on my parents' relationship. With strain came miscommunication. Then explosive arguments. The snowball seemed to never end. The pressure of raising us was starting to take its toll.

Money wasn't just tight; it was frequently nonexistent.

My mom took on as many jobs as needed. My father kept working at IBM and kept drinking. What looked like the "American work ethic" to a little boy quickly colored to the "American battle to stay afloat, both personally and within your relationships."

I was just a little boy at the time, and it was probably going on for much longer than when I eventually caught on.

My bedtime was consistently 7:30 or 8:00 p.m., no later. I liked the routine. Plus, I always had to get up early for Mass. During the day I would run around nonstop, so falling asleep was easy. But I was also a light sleeper, and the noises often kept me up much later than intended.

Screaming.

Crashing.

The angry sounds of parents fighting.

The lack of money . . .

. . . and my father's drinking.

It wasn't pretty—no parental fight is. What seemed like the middle of the night was really only 10:00. It didn't matter how many times it happened. I would sit up in bed, completely freaked out, and start crying and screaming. Invariably, my older brother Brian was the one to come and rescue me from my terror.

Too many times to count. I wanted it to all stop.

And eventually, it did. As time progressed, my dad drifted further away from us and further into the bottle. I would walk out of my bedroom to see a case—or cases—of beer stacked up outside his bedroom, not knowing when he got them or when he was coming out. To this day, I can't be sure of the demons my dad was mentally battling, but whatever they were, they were winning. And his heart was growing cold. I never worried that he didn't love us. I just worried about the dark side taking prominent reins.

What's the old adage? *April showers bring May flowers.* I was born in April, and as a Christian, that meant a good chance at having your birthday fall on Easter Sunday at least once in your life. It happened to me on my eighth birthday.

It was a warm spring day. Unusual for Erie because the chance of snow was ever present, even in April. But not that year. I can still picture the Easter Bunny cake my mom made for me with black licorice whiskers and jelly bean eyes. I loved it. After the cake was eaten and gifts were opened, we headed outside to play a game of family Wiffle ball. A perfect eighth birthday.

Except my dad was not there.

He was at the hospital.

The warmth of the day was replaced by the cold scene in the hospital room. The black jelly bean eyes of the Easter Bunny cake were replaced with my dad's hazel eyes.

Bloodshot.

I could see the struggle he was going through. This wasn't a metaphorical fight. He was lying down, strapped and restrained to his bed, struggling to excise the alcoholic demons from his body. He was in rehab, going through significant withdrawal.

I don't know how long it took, but his fight didn't end when he left the hospital. It was just the beginning. The "April showers" lasted well into May . . . and beyond. He did not return home. He moved out and lived alone in an apartment for years. My parents separated, but they did not divorce. They lived apart but stayed legally and sacramentally together till death did part them. We were Irish *Catholic*, remember?

Life changed for our family, but we were resilient. I watched and consumed the challenges of my parents' marriage, the familial changes, and my dad's battle with alcoholism and buried it deep inside.

I would often ask to stay with him so that he was not by himself. Just because he was struggling didn't mean he should have to be alone. I panicked over his isolation and couldn't help but imagine myself alone in his shoes. I knew my presence could be of comfort to him during this time. We were family. We shared a name. We shared a bond.

I had my little life and world under control.

Or so I thought.

There came a period of my childhood when it seemed I contracted every type of respiratory illness. My life was measured out by antibiotic after antibiotic. Every type of prescription and over-the-counter medicine ran through my veins. Kids getting sick was nothing new in a family of nine kids. One got sick, got better, another one got sick, got better, and on and on. End of story.

But for me, this was the beginning of a quiet, dark chapter in my life. My first exposure to the concept of being one's own worst enemy.

One night, while lying in bed and trying to fall asleep, I overheard my mother whispering to one of my brothers.

"I think all of those drugs and his months of sickness is making him behave this way."

I don't know if it was that, or the suppressed events of my early childhood, but something—other than the physical—was wrong. There's only so many medicines one can take before starting to wonder if the cause is really physical or psychological. Even at a young age, I couldn't help but wonder.

In the midst of whirlwind prescription bottles, my life had suddenly been invaded and overcome by severe anxiety. Pervasive thoughts of not being a good person ran through my head. The voices would pound on me over and over to the point where my body couldn't help but reflect the inner turmoil.

Where I internally panicked, I externally cried.

Where I couldn't calm my own thoughts, I trembled in fear.

As my mind raced into a dismal abyss, I became paralyzed in proper functionality in my day-to-day existence.

I couldn't go to school. I couldn't be social. I couldn't even be at home without the need to call someone for help. I did try going to school, but only a short time would pass before the anxiety, fear, and dark thoughts swirled in pure chaos. Too many times, my father had to leave work to come pick me up from school.

I couldn't stop my mind from going *there*. To the dark place.

I was convinced I was a *bad person*.

A *really* bad person.

And still to this day, I have no idea why. And neither did my parents. Did I feel responsible for my parents fighting and separating? Did I blame myself because his hospitalization was on my birthday? Should I have seen this coming? When I heard them fighting, should I have intervened? He was all alone in that apartment now; would he feel like we abandoned him? Did I feel abandoned?

My parents quickly sought professional help in the form of a counselor, and because I thought I was also maybe evil, I spent time with our parish priest. If a human counselor couldn't fix me, maybe God could.

Talking to outsiders was helpful, but this was a tough battle that no one could quite make heads or tails of. I was hoping for a quick fix. I had been on so many medications for my physical ailments, there had to be something just as easy for my mental and emotional ailments. An antibiotic for the soul. I wasn't sure how much more—or for how much longer—I could take.

I remember the breaking point like it was yesterday.

It was a cold, dreary, winter day. I had come home early from school because I just couldn't be there anymore without causing a disruption. Alone in the house, I lay in my bed, hoping to calm the chaotic inner voices of fear and self-loathing.

But I couldn't.

And I needed those thoughts to stop.

I got out of bed, placed my hands on both sides of the bedroom window frame, and gently pressed my head against the cold windowpane. Repeatedly, I lifted my head off the window and pressed against it over and over with a quickening pace.

Bang.

With each blow, I envisioned my body on the cement patio two stories below me.

Bang.

My intention was clear.

Bang.

I was going to put my head through the window and end it.

Bang.

With each progressively harder press and conclusive outcome, a red flag of reality suddenly presented itself. Yes, the dark and intrusive thoughts would end, but so would my life. It hadn't actually occurred to me that ending *it* also meant ending *my life*. Was I really ready to take this path and leave an empty hole within my family?

There were already eight kids ahead of me—maybe no one would care.

But I was the baby and the favorite, so of course they would care.

But I was such a burden on their time and energy, and even my mom thought something was wrong with me.

But did I really want to prove everyone right that there was something actually wrong with me?

"People who kill themselves are selfish," my mom would say when the mood struck. Her own experiences with her father and her faith created a stark, unbudging definition of suicide that didn't leave much room for today's nuances of mental health. But all I knew then was that I was miserable and in so much emotional and mental anguish.

But I wasn't selfish.

I didn't *want* to be selfish.

I pulled my head from the cold windowpane for the last time, sat on my bed, and told myself over and over again, "You're not selfish." This was my moment. This was my chance to let my will win out over the fear. I could be stronger than my own head.

If I could talk myself out of *this*, I could talk myself out of anything.

This was the first and last time the thoughts of ending my life ever got so far. But this was just one day amongst thousands. And I didn't want to be alone in it anymore. I knew help had to be found somewhere. I just wasn't sure where.

After that night, on the surface, I let it seem like little Jimmy was back to his old self and in control again, but the internal struggles hadn't gone anywhere. Sure, I'd talked myself off a literal ledge, but that resolve didn't wave a magic wand over every persistent thought.

I was in fifth or sixth grade by this point, still serving as an altar server. I found myself not only serving Mass but also turning to God. Maybe He could be the dose of perspective I'd been craving but hadn't yet found.

The daily struggles continued, but the pervasiveness of my internal war-zone was always worse at night. By this age, I essentially had my own room since so many of my other siblings had moved out or were in high school and out much later than my bedtime. The thoughts of being a bad person still screamed out at night against the quiet of the house. My mind raged on while my body grew exhausted from the anxious nature of my thoughts. Tears quietly running down my face, my body would give way to my mind, and I would eventually fall asleep.

The wash, rinse, and repeat nature of my bedtime routine was unsustainable. During one of my more tortuous nights, I decided enough was enough. I was angry, exhausted, and just ready to feel . . . normal again.

I could no longer just wait for God alone to help me. He wasn't a Magic 8 ball that I could shake enough times to produce quick, ready-made answers to my existential needs. If I was going to strengthen my resolve with the cross that I was apparently forced to carry, I needed to find a way to help myself. The answer was finally clear.

I was going to become a priest.

I would serve God at the ultimate level when I was older and able to join. If He wasn't going to help me at that moment, I would force my way into His immediate line of sight. I refused to be ignored.

I can't say that it happened that night, but a peaceful calm soon came over me. Any time the chaos in my mind revved up, I would immediately reconfirm that *I was going to become a priest* and my problems would be solved, and my mind would reset.

I took on a whole new persona. One that found ways to be kind and helpful to others. I would not let anything bother me. My family noticed a difference and was relieved that I was in a much better place, even though the tormenting thoughts continued. But now I had a way to control them.

I was going to become a priest.

My priestly thoughts were so prevalent in my mind that I began to portray my internal battle by publicly blessing myself. Mostly discreetly so as not to be showy, but I was occasionally caught in the act. Strangely, it was always when my brother Brian was around. He rescued me during my parents' fights, and now he was the one to bear witness to my public display of the sign of the cross.

"Jimmy, you alright bro?"

Yep. I was all good.

I was going to become a priest.

I was able to reset my thoughts with other thoughts. Never understanding how exactly it worked, I did not care. I leaned into this newfound safety net where I'd sit back and let my mind do all the heavy lifting to put itself at ease. If I could focus enough on the repeat of *You're going to become a priest . . . it will all be OK,* then I could convince myself that it would—indeed—all be OK.

I was going to become a priest.

This particular battle period in my early childhood lasted for approximately three years. I call it a "battle" because that's exactly how it felt. I was constantly at war with my own thoughts, emotions, anxieties, and temptations. How does a middle school kid convince himself so thoroughly he is a bad person that he's eaten alive by anxiety? I still have no idea how I got there, but I know that if I didn't allow myself to talk me out of it . . . my life would look very different.

The years went by, and the thoughts got quieter. Ever-present, but quieter.

I am not sure if my parents ever fully resolved the issues that put such strain on their marriage. My dad addressed his alcoholism, and as we all got older, there was relief from the financial burden. I can't remember when, but my dad eventually moved back into our house. It was a relief to have the family put back together again.

There was no question that my parents loved and took care of each other or that they loved and wanted to take care of us. Gone were the days when I would have to worry about my dad being alone in his apartment. We were under one roof. I had a strong bond with both of my parents.

By the time I was sent off to Cathedral Preparatory School, gone were the thoughts of *being a priest*. Sure, I was constantly surrounded by theological guidance that continued to help build my relationship with God, but I no longer felt the need to throw myself onto a path of vocational desperation.

Don't get me wrong, I'm no Holy Roller. I am a person who has made and will continue to make mistakes in life. But people have to look for strength somewhere. I barely understood the relationship between my own heart and mind, but I understood my relationship with God.

In my senior year of high school, we were instructed to make an album that defined to others who we were and our hopes and dreams for the future. There were many prompts for this assignment, but one particular prompt stood out.

Our greatest fear.

In the absolute center of an 8.5 x 11-inch piece of paper, a single, black, boldfaced word surrounded by nothing but the whiteness of the page that described my greatest fear in life then, and now:

ALONE!

How could someone with such a large extended family ever feel alone? It was definitely possible. While I was never numerically alone, I found that being alone triggered the negative thoughts that would override the balance in my heart and mind. The precarious balance in my head found the scales tip in favor of fear and anxiety. When I was physically overcome, usually at night, I would take myself out of bed and move to a distracting situation that would help me reestablish the balance.

As I moved away from my *I was going to become a priest* mantra, I had to relearn new strategies to talk myself out of my own head, which was not an easy concept. These episodes would happen randomly, but thankfully, not all the time.

There are a million and one things I could say about high school itself.

I had a growth spurt that took me to six foot three inches.

So, with my height and a bit of skill, I played basketball.

Which opened the door to having a decent number of dates.

Paid for by my job at a family-owned grocery store.

Where I met an array of interesting characters who would play roles later in my life.

The optics of my high school life eventually balanced with the internal demons that plagued years of my childhood. The older I got, the more manageable my anxiety. The more friends I made, the less ALONE! in the world I felt.

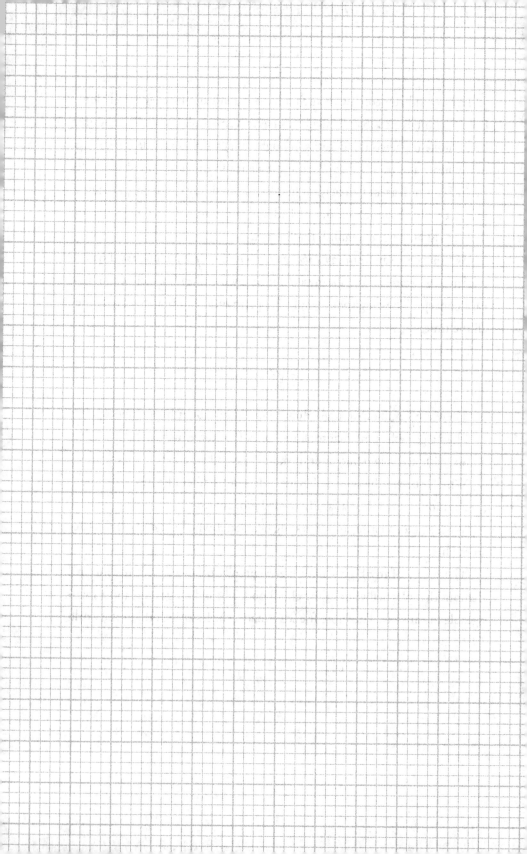

CHAPTER 3

Way 'Nough

To turn nothing into something is magic.

A mystery.

A miracle.

A masterstroke of hard work that I witnessed throughout my childhood.

By the time I finished high school, I felt like I was in pretty good control of my life. I was an expert at the headspace game. College was . . . a different story, at least at first.

I chose to attend Mercyhurst University just fifteen minutes from my house. The cost and commute benefits—not to mention the connection my family had with the Sisters of Mercy—outweighed any other option. It was a practical but depressing start.

Because I did not live on campus, I drove to school, took a few classes, and headed to either home or work. I didn't have a connection to anything or anyone. I watched as my classmates discussed weekend plans and post-class activities, none of which I was a part of. I was like a zombie meandering through my own life and watching it pass me by.

I wanted to get involved in sports. This was a small school, and I was a pretty good basketball player. I figured I had a good chance at securing a walk-on spot. I went to the gym with confidence and sized up the team and the coach, and I was going to make a play to join the team. I was six foot three, 180 pounds, with some good skills. I could make an impact.

That . . . never happened.

When you're tall, most people assume you play basketball. I assumed that's what I would play. My assumptions were proved wrong by some other huge dudes on campus.

The rowing team.

They picked me out from the crowd as I stood above pretty much everyone around me.

"Hey, do you know anything about rowing?" they asked on a random, life-changing day.

Outside of watching the Olympics every four years, I knew nothing about rowing. They said it did not matter.

"Do you like to work out? Drink beer?"

Absolutely.

They failed to mention that there was actually very little time to drink beer and that the sport itself was painfully difficult to execute and could mess with your mind. But it did not matter. I fell in love with the sport and the team. My new schedule was set: morning practices five days a week and races on the weekend. This routine set the standards for the next four years of my life and set me on a trajectory I never saw coming.

The team quickly found out that not only was I tall, but I was also strong and could haul a boat through the water. My technique on the other hand . . . was a work in progress. The freshman fall season of rowing was short. We traveled to a few races and competed against much larger schools. I was enamored by all of it.

The sport.

The competition.

The elite rowing powerhouses of the Ivy League.

The smell of the air over the water on a crisp autumn morning.

The whole culture of rowing consumed me. I had found my people in a community that didn't even exist in my world until that point.

$$\wedge\!\!\!\bigvee\!\!\!\wedge$$

Offseason for rowing was no joke. Lifting weights was the easy part; it was sitting on the rowing machine for countless hours, two times a day, just to produce what seemed like unachievable and incremental gains in our strength and endurance that was the most frustrating part. By the time spring season came around, I had grown another three inches and fifteen pounds of muscle. I had progressed enough that the coach thought it would be great to pull together a freshmen 4+ (four rowers plus a coxswain) to see how we would do.

I had no idea what to expect heading into the first race of the spring season. Our coxie—the team member responsible for commanding and steering the boat, Annie—was well trained and knew how to put us in our place and get us aligned.

Heading into the last week of practice prior to our first race, the boat was just not rowing well. We seemed to be working against each other, not maliciously or intentionally, just selfishly trying to perfect our own rowing stroke. Annie was great at giving us a bit of space to figure it out. Not too much space, but just enough so that we could, for a moment, move away from being raw power and brute force to being thoughtful and technique-focused rowers. But her patience with us did not last very long. She had had enough.

"Way 'nough!" she screamed.

This was the command to stop everything immediately and shut the boat down. She let us know she appreciated our attempt, but it wasn't working, and it was time to fall in line and listen. She quickly commanded us to all "sit ready." She was going to put us through a few 500-meter pieces to work out the kinks in our heads that were manifesting in our flow.

"Row!" she belted out.

She wanted 10 solid strokes to get the boat moving, and then we were going to settle into a 50-stroke sprint between 36–38 strokes per minute. With each stroke pounding through the water, we could feel the boat getting faster and faster. It felt amazing. We did it; we found our rhythm.

We were better, but not good enough.

"Way 'nough!"

We would do it all over again and again and again. Each time we *thought* we were doing better than the piece before.

Not quite.

Annie was looking for something particular from the boat and from us. We had one more 500-meter piece to complete. She said that she was pleased with the power, but there was something more she was looking for. Just prior to the piece, she said she was going to try a mental technique on us to help us get to where she wanted us to go, to be our best.

"Sit ready, row!"

Her voice echoed across the lake as she belted out what seemed to be a thousand commands in just a few strokes. Once the first ten strokes were out of the way, it was time to just crank it up.

"Shut your eyes."

What? Seriously? That was not a standard rowing command.

"Shut your eyes, now."

We listened. We were now rowing aggressively with our eyes closed, and we could feel the boat drifting into chaos.

"Now, imagine you're getting a blow job!"

What?!

That was *definitely* not a standard rowing command.

But we did as she commanded. The boat immediately set up, was balanced, and moved faster, more aggressively, and more relaxed than ever before. It was incredible.

"Way 'nough!"

We had just completed our fastest, most synchronized 500-meter piece of the practice. Annie was pumped. Splashing us with water like dogs in heat. Exhausted and out of breath, Annie got us rowing a light paddle back to the boathouse.

"That is how you row a boat and kick some ass, boys; we are going to be fine."

I was in disbelief.

"You all knew you had the muscular strength," she said. "Now I wanted you to experience the power of the mind. The expectation moving forward is to row and feel like you are getting a blow job: strong, hard, and relaxed."

It felt a bit ridiculous, but Annie wasn't wrong. This was my first experience with sports psychology. While I would not call it a *professional* lesson in mindset training (and quite frankly, an HR nightmare in the real world), it worked. We won gold in every race we competed in.

But it wasn't as relaxing or as easy as she made it out to be. During our first race, we felt unstoppable. We were going to row like Annie taught us, and we would be just fine. What we did not take into consideration was the outlier situations, the uncontrollable.

"Sit ready, row!"

The official belted out the command for the race to begin. We took five strokes to get the boat moving and then another powerful ten strokes to break away from the pack. We were cruising.

That is, until I caught a crab.

"Catching a crab" is when the rower's oar gets sucked under the water, presumably by a crab or just because of poor rowing technique. I was still a novice, and my technique was not perfect. Our boat speed and momentum were shutting down. The other crews pulled away from us. Annie screamed out.

"Fix it Jim, get your oar back in the oar lock, let's go!"

Shit. That certainly was *not* how a blow job was supposed to feel.

We were 250 meters behind. My catching of a crab was publicly announced for the spectators to hear on shore, and our boat was dead last by mid-race. I quickly regrouped and we were back on. It was time to be strong, hard, and relaxed. I needed to clear my mind of my own stupid mistake and overcome the adversity we were facing. Annie calmed us, or me, down with some encouraging words, and it was on.

With every stroke, Annie could see we were catching up to one boat at a time; this too was being publicly announced. Our boat was coming back from the dead in a crazy push for the last 500 meters. We ended up winning by 100 meters, and we walked away with our first gold medal.

Nirvana was reached.

We would wash, rinse, and repeat this process the entire spring season.

The next season of rowing came as quickly as the first ended. I was pumped—I would no longer be the novice on the team. I made the varsity program and was awarded a small scholarship. I was now *officially* a collegiate athlete.

With the new set of freshmen, a whole new vibe enveloped the team. We were going to be more competitive. We were going to work even harder. I was pushing my body and mind in ways I'd never imagined. After years of childhood mental anguish, my brain reveled in the elite focus on something other than myself.

My body . . . not so much.

It turned out that growing three inches, gaining fifteen pounds of muscle, and competing in an aggressive sport takes a toll on one's lower back.

In the midst of an autumn race before packing up for winter training, I felt my lower back pop and seize up. It was a full-blown muscle spasm. The pain was incredible, and I could not properly get out of the boat. I ended up rolling my body out of the boat and onto the docks. I went straight to the sports medicine office on campus to confirm what I already knew: it was indeed a really bad muscle spasm.

But there was something else going on that required a more intensive look. By this point, it was nearly impossible for me to complete the simple tasks of the day. I could not bend over to get my pants on or get in and out of a car. I made a ninety-year-old look young and vibrant. The disks in my lower back, or the vertebrae in the lumbar and sacral regions (L4, L5, S1), were bulging, but thankfully not ruptured.

I had fallen in love with the sport, built new relationships, built a new body . . . and it broke. I had taught myself long ago as a kid not to wallow in self-pity, and damn it if that was going to all fall to pieces with a little back pain. I set out to return to the water as soon as possible. Mind over matter and all, right?

The grueling winter training program was replaced by three months of intensive physical therapy. Erg and weight training were replaced with hours of traction, electrical stimulation, walking in a circular pool against a four-miles-per-hour current, and the use of the stationary bike to strengthen my back.

I lost my seat in the boat for the spring season because I couldn't complete the winter training. My sophomore year of rowing was officially over.

I remained as much of an active member of the team as possible without setting myself back. This kept my heart in the sport and fed my mind's appetite for order by having a system in place to overcome my latest challenge. I don't know if my teammates cared one way or another, but to me, it was a psychological necessity. If I stepped away completely just to focus on rehab with no connection to the team, I feared I would return to the place I feared most in the world.

Being ALONE!

By the end of the spring season, I felt amazing. I was stronger, more flexible, and more resilient. I built great new relationships with the new rowers and began to take on a leadership role within the program. As things started to shape up for my junior year, we learned that our coach was resigning and new leadership would be coming in the fall.

The new coach brought a whole different level of training to the program. The competition was going to be great. By some nonrowing stroke of luck, I was selected as team captain for my junior and senior years. Just two years prior I had never even taken a stroke. I wasn't the fastest rower or the best, but it was my effort, mindset, and heart that made the difference. I was there even when I couldn't participate. I showed up even though my seat was lost. My efforts, it turned out, did not go unnoticed.

Rowing is a physically and mentally grueling sport. The amount of energy and effort exuded during a 2,000-meter race has been said to be equivalent to playing two full-court basketball games in roughly seven minutes. This level of fitness does not happen overnight. We pounded the rowing machines for hours at a time just to make incremental gains. Every couple of weeks, we would reassess by painfully completing another 2,000-meter erg test.

When I first started rowing, the test took me 6 minutes and 58 seconds. Not to toot my own horn, but apparently, breaking seven minutes was a big deal for new rowers. It took me the next three years to drop forty seconds to have an erg score of 6:18. The first twenty seconds seemed to melt away faster than butter in a hot pan; the next twenty seconds fell off at a glacial pace.

Under the new coach, every aspect of winter training was scrutinized to maximize output and minimize concerns for overtraining. We wore heart rate monitors to ensure staying within the defined heartbeats-per-minute range. Every beat was watched and recorded so as not to deviate from the plan.

While there was a monitor for the heart, there wasn't one for the mind. I had to find ways to win the battle against the rowing machine during each practice. Goals were laid out prior to the start of each practice so you would know how much pain and mental torment you would be going through. When it felt completely impossible to keep going, we had to tell ourselves to push harder. My old mantra of *You're going to become a priest* to distract my invasive thoughts was replaced by *Just one more stroke.* It sounds a bit like a torture chamber, but we fed off the pressure.

We loved it.

I loved it.

Just one more stroke.

By the middle of my junior year, there were miraculously no signs of any lingering back issues. I was in the best shape of my life and feeling great. Winter training was tough, but we made it through together. Each hour spent sweating it out on the erg got us closer to being able to take some strokes on the water.

Just one more stroke.

Our new coach was pleased. We were all executing as required. Deviation was not tolerated. My mind was sharp, and I was winning the battle on the erg while the heart monitor would let the coaches and coxies know how my physical progress was going. I was controlling the controllable.

Just one more stroke.

As winter training progressed, staying within the defined heart rate range was relatively simple. If it started to slip, you just had to make the appropriate change in effort on the rowing machine. It was easily correctable.

For me, I needed to consistently stay within 130–135 beats per minute over the course of each of the workout pieces. Easy. Simple. A muscle-rendering piece of cake.

Until it wasn't.

Just one more stroke.

The heart rate monitors were connected to the screens on our ergs for the viewing pleasure of our coaches and coxies. Rowing is a rhythm sport. It takes a lot of energy, effort, and technique to get into a good space, but once achieved, the flow can continue as long as you control your body and, more importantly, your mind.

I would break up the hundreds and thousands of strokes into equal parts and focus on some portion of the stroke. Ten or twenty strokes for legs, ten or twenty strokes for back, for hands away, for quick catches, etc.

Just one more stroke.

During a routine practice, my heart started playing some sneaky little tricks on me. With my ass on the erg, during the umpteenth workout piece of the day, my mind and body in the flow state, I started to feel anxious. It was odd. Something was off.

Just one more stroke.

The heart monitor captured everything and reported that I was no longer in the 130–135 bpm workout range; I was 20–30 beats over that.

"'Sup with that, Jimmy?" my coxie asked.

I wasn't sure.

I hadn't changed anything about my stroke, effort, or rhythm. I was in a flow. But now other eyes in the room were on me and my mind game was shot. My anxiety started to rise even higher, and my body reacted. And just like that, my heart rate snapped right back to 130–135 bpm.

"Interesting," my coxie said. "Might be a heart monitor issue. Get the swing back, you have eighteen minutes to go."

Just one more stroke.

After a normal completion of practice, I kept hearing my coxie's words over and over again.

"It's probably a monitor issue."

I wanted to believe that. I didn't want to start worrying about something that was not there.

But I *felt* it. It was physical to me, or it was mental, or both.

I felt my heart switch gears and then downshift. Did it rev up because of my mind, or did my mind rev up because I felt my heart switch? I knew I could play mind games with myself—that was nothing new—but I did not think I could mentally control the on-and-off switch of my heartbeat. I decided to move on. I wasn't going to spiral over something that wasn't there. There was *nothing* there.

"It's probably a monitor issue."

Just one more stroke.

A few weeks passed. It was another nondescript, lengthy practice. We were all in the flow and feeling good. We were only a few weeks away from heading off for spring break. The coaches and coxies were in a good mood. Until my heart jumped up forty beats.

Shit. It was happening again. I was covered in a hot sweat, and, if possible, I started feeling a cold sweat on top of it.

"What the hell is that, Kaveney?"

The endearing "'Sup with that, Jimmy?" from my coxie was replaced with the more intense, vitriolic tone of my coach. I had committed the greatest of training sins: I deviated from the training plan. You would have thought I committed some heinous crime by his tone and expression.

The other coaches and coxies swarmed around me.

"Correct it, now! Do you think you are special? Are you better than the team?"

They thought that I was showing off and my heart monitor was reflecting my showmanship.

What the hell?

My effort did not change; my strokes per minute and split did not change. Everything was working as planned. Everything except my heart.

What seemed to last thirty minutes was all over in about thirty seconds. Through no restraint or aggressive change in my performance, it all just . . . stopped. Within the blink of an eye, I went from 175 bpm right back down to 130 bpm.

"Good recovery," said my coach. He walked away, and there was no further discussion.

These cardiac anomalies continued on and off for the rest of my college rowing career. I was a well-trained athlete and managed this situation as I did with most things: bury it deep inside and address it later if it became a greater problem.

Just one more stroke.

Or something like that.

I would like to say that my rowing career finished up the way it started, with lots of gold medals and resounding success.

It didn't.

At this point in my college's rowing history, we were the fastest, biggest, and strongest crew ever assembled. We were rowing strong and hard but not relaxed. We needed Annie to get our minds straight about what a blow job should feel like.

Our hearts were in it; our minds were not. At the very least, we helped elevate the rowing program and laid the foundation for future crews and multiple national championships for both the men's and women's teams.

College graduation came with the senior athletic dinner, every commencement possible, and all the other end-of-year nonsense. I relished it. Four years prior, I had no idea what I was going to do with my college career. Whether it was fate or the hand of God—I believe the latter—a path was laid out for me. Options and opportunities were presented, and choices were made.

Some good, some bad. At this point, I planned to focus on the good and not hold onto the things I regretted.

Rowing changed my life. As I walked away from the competitive side at the end of my college career, I knew rowing was now in my DNA. I would never look at another body of water without wondering what it would be like to feel that water gliding underneath my rowing shell.

But, somehow, after all this direction to get through school and find something I was forever passionate about, I wound up in the exact same place as when I started. I had no idea what was to come, and everyone could see right through me.

At the athletic banquet, the coaches from each sport had a moment to say something inspiring to their graduating seniors. I listened to the thoughtful comments aimed at others . . . and then my name was called. I heard a quick summary of my rowing accomplishments, and my coach paused, unsure of what to say *inspirationally*.

"Jim Kaveney, the world is your oyster."

The words seemed to bounce off the walls of the banquet hall over and over, echoing in the ears of everyone in front of me. After listening to the thoughts about everyone before me, with direction and purpose, these words cut deep. He was suggesting I had unlimited opportunities with a bright future. But my interpretation was more in line with: You are directionless—no additional schooling, no big job to jump into.

Good luck.

**CHAPTER 4**

The Taste of Entrepreneurship

I was going to be a doctor.

No!

A physical therapist.

No!

A hospital administrator.

During high school, biology was the only advanced placement course I took. I struggled but got through it. My teacher did not think too highly of me. In fact, when I shared with her that I was going to be a biology major in college, her last words to me were condescending.

"Wow, I hope you figure out how to study and learn."

Three cheers for encouraging young, impressionable minds . . .

But I loved science. On any given day during college, it was debatable which of my two loves took priority.

Rowing or science.

Science or rowing.

I ended up as only one of eight biology majors to graduate in my class, but the path to my degree was not exactly straight. For the life of me, I couldn't figure out what I wanted to *do* with my degree. At the end of the day, I graduated with a general biology degree. Nothing truly inspired me. I'd never had that glorious "ah-ha" moment that so many others seemed to experience. Then it hit me.

I would become a biology teacher.

My mother loved teaching. I could follow in her steps. At the time, there was a high demand for male science teachers. I could do that. Sure, I would have to come back to school after graduation and get certified to teach. It would be another three semesters of schooling. That was fine. I did not think I was ready to get out into the real world yet.

We were a relatively small school, so I had the pleasure of interacting with the president of the college many times. He knew I was going to be graduating and continuing with my education degree to hopefully teach biology. There was finally some direction, but he also knew I was a bit confused about . . . everything.

"Jim, if you truly follow your heart, the rest of it, and money, will follow. Figure out what you love."

While I chose to pursue additional credits to become a teacher, I still was not quite sure it was for me. But, at this point in my career, I made the choice, and I was going to see it through. I was twenty-two years old, but my mind was not ready for what was to come. It could have been because my heart did not attach to something specifically. I thought I *loved* science, but I felt like I was settling for a path that seemed, well, *un*loved . . . by me, at least.

I had some growing up to do.

Right as I was beginning my postgraduate work in biology education, I got my second taste of entrepreneurship.

The first taste was with my brother Brian when he started Kaveney Brothers Painting. I was a bit young at the time to fully be a work mule, but he let me join in on the fun by cleaning paintbrushes and moving around equipment. The few bucks he would throw at me here and there was an added bonus. The *Kaveney Work Ethic* was full steam ahead with Brian, who later went on to build another business. But when the time came, and I was more age appropriate, Brian's path was a bit outside of my wheelhouse. So, instead, I got behind the wheel.

My older brother Tommy was in transportation, logistics, and trucking. There wasn't a truck he didn't love and moving freight, large and small, to and fro, is what he did best. There was no such thing as a "logistical nightmare" for him. He was an expert at this and at working with people.

Watching him build his business, TJ Kourier, from scratch was inspiring. Based out of Erie, Pennsylvania, Tommy and his business came home, and my parents were ecstatic to have another one of their kids back in the nest.

Not knowing much about trucking, I really had no clue what was required. All I saw was what happened on the road. I had no idea what work was taking place behind the scenes or the ideas running in his mind. All I knew was he had a huge heart for trucks and people, one of which was his baby brother.

Even though I had some postgraduate work to help pay for the extra tuition for my teaching license, it wasn't quite enough to cover the bills. It was the late 1990s, and my brother offered ten dollars per hour to drive trucks for him in the evening. No sweat.

He started his business with one twenty-two-foot box truck and his Ford Taurus station wagon. The truck would be a bit too big for me to drive, so I was relegated to the station wagon until he bought a cargo van. His first account was hauling industrial-sized saw blades from Erie, Pennsylvania, to Akron, Ohio. A five-hour round trip. I would leave between 4:30 and 5:00 p.m. and get back just in time to hit the bars . . . or go to sleep. I drove this route three or four times a week for a while. The money was decent, and I watched my big brother turn his passion into a steady flow of business.

As time went on, his business grew faster than expected, and more than once he asked me to stay on. Help him grow it. He knew it was going to be big. He had the heart and mind for trucking.

I . . . did not.

It was fun helping him for a while, but I was still planning my career in education. That was my focus. That is what I thought was my one true love, and so I was following *my* heart.

Each of my siblings thought I had lost my mind. As his business grew, I was the only one in the family he asked to join him. Out of all nine, I was his "chosen one." We were the most similar. My siblings were doing their own thing and watching the business grow from a distance. But me? How could I turn down such a sure thing?

But I just couldn't say *yes*. It did not feel right to me.

My mind was made up. Finish schooling, get certified to teach biology, and go make a career of it.

Except, there were two problems.

One, at a time when male science teachers were supposedly in demand, I could not actually find a full-time job.

Two, I had seen the future me teaching through the lens of my practicum teachers' experiences. I saw the future, and it did *not* look good.

At the end of my career, I did not want to ask what could have been. I wanted no regrets. I was working with two very nice men, equally smart and dedicated to their profession, but I listened as they both bemoaned in regret at not doing something different with their lives. One teacher was more dynamic than the other. But my direct supervisor was literally using the same lesson plan that he had written twenty years prior.

Holy shit.

I could not do that.

The more I thought of future me, the more I felt the walls of the classroom enclose and crush my spirit. I know, I know. His experience did not have to be mine. But I just felt that there was something else I should be doing. At this point, I hardly knew which way was up anymore. All the time and effort and work and money spent to become a teacher. And I just . . . didn't want it anymore.

The world was my oyster, and I now found myself wanting to see how that tasted.

While I worked to figure everything out, I took on substitute teaching during the day (which thankfully required less commitment and more flexibility) and continued to drive for my brother at night. I was living at home, so the cost of room and board wasn't really an issue. Three square meals a day and a consistent roof over my head. By my siblings' standards, my life was easy. But this floating aimlessly through life wasn't good for my mind.

I watched my friends take on incredible jobs with significant salaries. My brother kept asking me to join his company. TJ Kourier was growing even more, and new opportunities were coming his way. And my same answer would return.

Happy to help when I could, but I needed to blaze my own trail.

My mind continued to spin looking for a sign, divine intervention, *something* to point me in the right direction. Unfortunately, it did not matter what I pursued; my heart didn't want to attach to anything. And nothing came from my efforts.

In today's world, they call it *millennial ennui*.

Or *Gen Z disengagement*.

I didn't suffer from ennui, and I certainly craved workplace engagement. But that was just it. That was the problem.

Sure, I could logically look at my situation, finances, and education and *talk* myself into taking a job. I could have been a biology teacher if I really wanted to. I could have easily settled into the *Kaveney Work Ethic* alongside my brother and helped him grow his trucking business. Hell, I could have been a delivery driver, a stock boy, a phone operator, anything.

But I didn't want to settle. I didn't want to have to talk myself into a job that my heart wasn't in. It may sound selfish or privileged or downright ridiculous. It may sound like a naïve twenty-something kid who hasn't had to truly face the real world yet.

But I wasn't selfish.

Definitely not privileged.

Sometimes ridiculous in college, but certainly not in my career aspirations.

And naïve? Maybe. But I knew with every fiber of my being that I needed purpose in a job beyond a paycheck. I craved to be passionate about how I spent my time and energy. Call it what you want.

I call it heart.

Like an epiphany, a sign presented itself. An old customer from my grocery store days was working out at the same gym as me.

"Jim, how the hell are you? What are you up to?"

The dreaded question for someone still soul-searching.

I gave him only the pertinent details about my biology degree and teaching and told him that I was looking into all related professional fields. He did not have much to say except the boilerplate statement: "I am sure something will come your way. You're talented."

Yeah, thanks.

It wasn't quite "the world is your oyster," but it rang eerily familiar. He wished me well and continued his workout. After several minutes, he stopped again, a little more out of breath.

"Thought of something, I don't really know her well, but my new sister-in-law is a bigwig at a large pharmaceutical company, maybe she could help you out. Send me your resume and I will get it to her."

One of my other brothers, Bill, was in pharma, and he loved it. He always talked about how he liked the marriage of his science background and sales. I hadn't ever really considered it a possibility for myself before that moment. Bill was so charismatic and so smart. I guess you could say there was just a touch of imposter syndrome.

But for the first time in a long time, I was fired up.

Within twenty-four hours, I turned over my resume and he immediately shipped it off to his new sister-in-law, Laura.

My fingers were crossed.

Within a week, I got an email. While I did not have a lot of experience, Laura liked the choices I was making. She wanted to meet me in person. She was going to be in Erie for Thanksgiving. *Awesome.*

Except . . .

Thanksgiving was a couple of months away.

An eternity.

But I waited.

And worked.

And waited some more.

When we finally met, we talked about the opportunities at her company. Because it was near the end of the year, they were going into a hiring freeze for the next six months.

Another eternity.

But Laura promised to circulate my resume to a few of the managers in my area. She advised me to stay in touch and, in the meantime, go get some sales experience.

Right.

Like it was easy.

The job search raged on, but the opportunities in our town were drying up. There was only so much to do in Erie. A friend of mine recommended we take a fresh look down South. So, we each packed up a suit, a couple of dress shirts and ties, and jumped into the car.

We did a road trip interview blitz through North and South Carolina, staying with college friends along the way. This turned out to be an exceptionally productive trip for picture books, memories, and the consumption of beer. But the dividends of our efforts stopped there.

The multitude of interviews was a dead end.

We finally returned north of the Mason-Dixon Line to continue the search locally.

Within a few weeks of each other, we both landed jobs in Cleveland.

This was it.

I was actually going to grow up, move out, and take on the world.

Move over oyster—Jim Kaveney was coming for you.

This was my first step toward gaining sales experience. I landed a job working for a recruiting company, a job placement center for computer professionals. We were inching closer to the end of the twentieth century and the internet was just starting to take off. This was the right place to be. This was cutting edge. This was my big break.

I lasted three months.

I was putting in sixty to seventy hours a week and making less money than when I was driving trucks and substitute teaching. Having been raised with the *Kaveney Work Ethic*, the long workdays did not phase me.

What phased me was the strange *cult*ure that made me question my longevity with the company. Every morning, usually around 7:30 or 8:00, we circled up in the center of the office. A bell would ring. Someone would scream out what they were working on for the day and why they loved working there. At first, I thought it was some weird hazing ritual for the new guy in the office.

At about two months in, the circle time was very much *not* just a fluke. At that point, I hadn't had the opportunity to participate in the circle, so, for no particular reason one Monday morning, I decided it was my time to sarcastically shine. I stepped out of the circle and rang the bell, indicating it was my turn.

"I actually don't have a pending request right now, but I just wanted to say how *awesome* it is to work with all of my peers. And how happy I am to be here."

Nobody caught my sarcasm, but they caught my energy and fed off it immediately.

Oops.

I sat down at my desk and looked across to my desk mate, Tony.

"We need to talk." This time, my tone was not so energetic.

Tony was my one friend at the company. He was right in line with my thinking about the company culture too. But he had been there for years and had a plan to execute before he left. He helped me make my decision to leave. After a few hours of discussing it with him, I was escorted out of the building because I was causing others to question their own place at work at the company.

I was a *liability*.

I drove back to my apartment, and with the distance, I felt a sense of relief. I had no other job lined up, but leaving felt better than staying.

I was young.

No family to think about.

No true responsibilities.

I was willing to take the risk.

For better or worse, this became my modus operandi moving forward.

Since I did not own a personal computer, I took up residency at the local library and pumped out resume after resume. I *needed* to get sales experience; Laura had told me so.

I also needed money, so I went back to work for my brother, driving trucks full time until something else hooked my heart. Periodically, I landed an interview with a pharmaceutical company, but they never panned out.

A few months later, I accepted an outside sales job with one of the largest office supply companies in the country. My role was to go up and down every street in my sales territory and call on any business with anywhere from one to a hundred employees. I had to dress in a suit and tie, which honestly fit my style. I felt comfortable dressing up. I should have been born in the roaring twenties.

I knocked on hundreds of doors.

I scoured the streets looking for prospective customers wanting to save money.

I was in charge of bringing to the masses top-tier office supplies: staples and printer cartridges.

I was . . . less than thrilled.

But it was new, and I was new to it, and the world was *my* oyster, damn it.

Sure, I craved passion, but I was also no quitter. I loved talking to people and I loved closing a deal. I just didn't love printer cartridges. Is that so crazy?

Quite frequently, the job took me into a doctor's office because they of course need office supplies for administrative tasks. All those obnoxious forms you need to fill out every time you walk into a doctor's office, guess what they need? Ink from a printer. And I was the guy to ensure full cartridges every time. And of course, I had to dress the part to sell the parts.

"Go ahead back to the sample closet, hun." My reverie over staplers and reams of paper was interrupted by the receptionist. "The doctor will see you shortly."

Samples?

Doctor?

I was not a drug rep, but apparently, I looked the part. A suit and tie could go a long way in the workplace. I was both thrilled and dejected. I knew I could make it work in pharma; I even had the outfit to match the role. But my outfit could only take me as far as the sample closet. It couldn't get me an interview without sales experience.

I could do it. I knew I could. At the very least, I did a really good job of telling myself I could. I just had to keep my head down, my tie on tight, and my office supply sales numbers high.

After six months at the company, I was inevitably restless. Sure, I was doing a fine job. But like trucking, my passion for office supplies just wasn't there. My heart yearned for something to challenge and inspire me. My head vacillated between the bills needing to be paid and my latest go-to mantra of *I could do it.*

My boss started to notice my malaise. She started spending extra time with me to observe and assess my performance. She was driven, obnoxiously driven. She kept telling me that I needed to gain some courage and get into every office. She couldn't understand why I didn't see dollar signs up and down every road that I traveled. She instructed me on how to only call on offices on the *right* side of the road because it was more efficient than waiting to cross traffic to get to an office on the *left* side.

Her hair was huge. Her beautifully painted—but far too long—fingernails would clickety-clack on any surface she could touch.

Yes.

I was judging her.

But she had officially gotten under my skin. During one of her last visits with me, she hit me with another bit of motivation to get into the offices and get the sale.

"Build your confidence, Jim, and when you see the 'no soliciting' sign, know that this is Italian for 'come on in.'"

Gross.

I was done.

I could not do it anymore.

Sales were *clearly* not for me.

Correction.

Office supplies sales were clearly not for me.

It sucked.

It sucked extra when the thing you were selling wasn't something of value. It wasn't like there was absolutely no inherent value to office supplies because, obviously, they serve a purpose. But no one's life was changing based on the brand of staples or the ply of printer paper they used. And if there was a way in which someone's life could change from office supplies, upper management definitely kept it a secret. I had no buy-in for what I was supposed to be selling people.

My heart wasn't in it.

So, I resigned.

And once again, I relied on my brother and his never-ending and generous offer to drive his trucks.

A few more months passed.

I still hadn't given up all hope for a job in pharmaceuticals. I did not like office supplies sales, but the question of pharma sales kept popping up in my mind. Printer cartridges versus lifesaving medicine. Staples versus disease prevention. It felt like a no-brainer and an all-hearter.

I still loved science. Pharma. Biotech. The human body in general. I could *see* myself in those spaces. I just couldn't manage to actually manifest myself in those spaces.

More months.

And countless interviews.

Followed by never-ending rejections.

I was exhausted and it was starting to show.

At one point, I was going on so many interviews that I screwed up big time. I received a call late on a Friday from a hiring manager. She wanted me to come in for these interviews she was hosting on Monday at one of the local hotels. She stated her name and the company's name. I hung up the phone and immediately went to the library. I spent a significant amount of time researching the company, the pipeline, and the opportunity.

I could do it.

Dressed for success, I drove to the hotel on Monday morning. There was a sign on the front desk indicating that interviews for the pharma company were in the ballroom and someone would be with you shortly.

I broke out in a cold sweat. I opened my folder and looked at the company I researched. *That* company name did not match the company on the sign. I asked the desk clerk if I was at the right hotel. I was. I was also sitting on all this information I researched about the wrong company.

I was escorted to the ballroom for my interview. The woman was quite pleasant, and then the first question came.

"Tell me what you know about our company."

I laughed out loud and told her about the mix-up. She also laughed, sat back, and said: "Well, you drove this far . . . tell me about our competition."

Shit.

Even though we both chuckled at the mistake, it was not going well. I drove home, stayed in my suit, dropped on my bed, and fell asleep.

I was tired.

Tired of the process.

Tired of no results.

Tired of being too tired to even get the company name right.

Maybe I created the mess myself because I could not figure out, for the longest time, what I wanted to do. By that point, I was twenty-five years old. I had finished my undergrad degree in biology three years prior and my postgrad program a year and a half prior.

By my own standards, I felt like a highly educated loser. The oysters of the world started to taste a bit rotten.

I ultimately moved back home to live with my parents and stayed until I was twenty-seven.

I know, I know.

There is a stigma surrounding grown men who move back in with Mom and Dad.

But why?

My parents were awesome and understood what was happening in my life. They offered me a welcoming landing place to get my head on straight and gather my bearings. There was no shame, no judgment. Just a whole lot of support and even more love.

Not to mention a whole lot of money saved from not having to pay rent with essentially zero income to back it up.

They liked having me back in the house. We often ate dinner together, and there was a mutual respect for my comings and goings, both professional and social. They put no pressure on me and "how long I was going to be there." I was allowed to figure it all out myself, in my time, as needed.

But . . . that damn *Kaveney Work Ethic.*

Something was going to break and soon. And it was going to either be a good break or a bad one. I could feel it. I could feel my mind starting to play tricks on me again. I needed to control it. I needed some sort of direction.

A purpose.

Thankfully, my heart would come through for me.

CHAPTER 5

Follow Your Heart

B oy meets girl.

Boy and girl become friends.

But *only* friends. Great friends.

Boy and girl date other people.

Until one fateful party when boy and girl look sideways at each other and can't help but wonder . . .

What if?

The nineties' rom-com enthusiasts might be tempted to accuse me of stealing from their favorite movie. But this was no movie.

This was Lisa.

While moving home was humbling, it gave me the opportunity to focus on other aspects of my life. I have always been known as the "mayor," the "glue" amongst all my friends. Let it be grade school, high school, or college,

I would always be in touch with people, ensuring everyone was connected. Chalk it up to my greatest fear of being ALONE!, but staying connected and connecting dots was something I was good at. And in a season of life where I had nothing but rejection after rejection, I held onto the thing I knew I could do.

Connecting with people.

The universe was finally on my side.

When I met Lisa, it was all thanks to mutual friends. In my efforts to stay connected with our closest out-of-state friends, Holly and Chopper, Lisa came into my life, and we—eventually—started dating.

She was beautiful and smart and funny and kind and gainfully employed. Fully independent.

And, well . . . I wasn't.

But that did not matter. I could feel my heart falling deeper for her, and as it should, my mind started thinking about potential long-term prospects. My job search was intense already, but I needed to pick up the pace if I ever wanted to make this relationship go somewhere further.

The summer with her was incredible. As the season started shifting to fall, I still had no job.

No opportunities.

Nothing.

Nada.

Zip.

But as the cold wind began to blow off the lake and the leaves began to change, so did my job search. I started getting more interviews, and given that I was now a professional interviewer, my conversations with potential employers turned from potential opportunities to true prospects.

On top of these leads, my original contact in pharma, Laura, came calling. I had kept in touch with her throughout my journey, and she held true to her word and called me back when her company lifted the hiring freeze.

Within a few short days of one another, I had two real job opportunities in front of me.

My spirits were lifted. I could feel the tides shifting in my favor. There was just one little problem.

Both job opportunities were outside of Erie.

I would have to move.

Again.

Lisa.

I was panicking. I had tried living in Cleveland, and that was a crap shoot. What if one of these places was no different? I knew I needed one of these jobs, but the thought of doing it on my own, without anyone, was terrifying.

I hated the idea of being ALONE!

I hated the idea of trying and failing yet again.

I hated the idea that not even trying could be considered failure.

I hated the idea of potentially having to choose one side of my heart for another. I *finally* felt like my heart was in it this time career-wise. But man, oh man, my heart was definitely in it relationship-wise.

I knew I was serious about my relationship, but this kind of move . . . I wasn't sure if it would stand the test of commitment. I would have to ask the question.

Lisa.

She knew I needed to accept one of these job offers. She had watched my mental and emotional struggle over finding a job. This was it. Deep breaths.

"I need to do this. I need to take on one of these opportunities. So I need to know if you are coming with me or not."

I couldn't dance around the point. There was no time for dancing, just work and love. My heart and my heart.

The commitment was there.

Her answer was short and direct.

"Yes. I am ready to follow you and do this together."
Lisa.

One of the jobs offered was to be a territory floater. Basically, that meant moving from city to city to across the country as needed, filling in where there was a vacancy. Seemed like a cool way to see the country. But it also seemed a bit unstable.

Laura's company was a local sales territory forty-five minutes away from Erie. During the interview process, I was told that I would need to live in the territory, otherwise it would be a deal-breaker.

This was not as attractive because my territory was technically "rural." Not a lot of thriving towns to choose from.

But *I could do it.* I would make it work. We would make it work together.

Just as fast as these two options appeared, one of them disappeared. The traveling sales job was put on the back burner. It was October, the fourth quarter, and the company decided to hold tight till January.

While it wasn't as bad as an outright "no," it was a big delay. I only had one real prospect left. I had my final interview in Rochester, New York. I needed to nail it.

I interviewed with two managers that day. I was sailing through the interview when they threw the promotional materials for one of their therapeutic medicines on the table.

"You have ten minutes to review the sales aid and give us a presentation."

I felt my core body temperature rising. I knew this was a sales job, a *scientific* one at that, but my anxiety about selling office supplies came rushing back.

Where Lady Macbeth saw phantom blood, I looked down at my shaking hands and saw phantom printer ink. I couldn't handle the turmoil of talking myself back into a role that my heart wasn't committed to.

I had told myself that I did not think office sales were for me. Was that true here too?

Well, it was a bit late in the game for full-on panic.

Laura was my mentor and had put her name on the line for me, so I had to pull this off. The ten minutes of prep time came and went, and it was time to show them what I was made of. Show myself what I was made of.

It wasn't the smoothest of presentations, to say the least, but my ability to communicate (and pronounce) the scientific aspects of the product without any formal training was pretty good. My biology degree came through for me at last.

All the time and money invested in my education and in myself would start to pay dividends. I told a coherent story and closed for the sale.

Done.

They told me that overall the presentation was really good, only a few bumps and bruises, but nothing a little training couldn't fix. I could easily be trained. If the right emotional foot were forward, I would take everything they gave me and not just run with it; I would sprint.

With a wink and a nod of approval, the interview wrapped. They told me to look forward to a phone call in the next few days. The hiring process was over, and I was *the man*, and this was going to move fast.

The phone call came.

The offer was accepted.

The feeling that took over my body was very similar to when I first started rowing. It just felt *right*. Like I belonged.

It was a little over three years from when I graduated to the time I got a job that I truly felt connected to. The journey to get to that point was not easy. I was sure the experiences would teach me some kinds of lessons for later in life. Probably something about staying the course, believing in yourself, not settling, *blah blah blah*.

But at that point, I was exchanging the smell of diesel fuel for the sweet menu the world was about to give me, and that's all that mattered.

Hello, oyster. My old friend.

CHAPTER 6

No Selling for You

To say that the hiring process was going to move fast is an understatement. It was the middle of October, and I was to start home-study training the first week of November with live corporate training taking place over three weeks right after Thanksgiving and before Christmas. I'd be rocking and rolling around the Christmas tree faster than I could blink.

I was hired in the middle of a pay period, so my first paycheck would be half of my two-week, take-home pay.

It was huge.

$685.00 after taxes.

I just won the lottery. I had never seen a check that large before in my life. Feeling rich and grateful, I did what any person would do with that kind of money—I spent it. I bought my mom a new dress, Lisa some clothes, and took my parents and Lisa out to dinner. To be able to say "my treat" and not secretly panic afterward about the money spent was a feeling like no other.

I was full of gratitude and love. Things were *finally* matching up to what I had always envisioned for myself.

The training was rigorous, but I loved every minute of it. I was putting my biology degree to work, and my teaching skills soon kicked in. I was one of fifty-five salespeople from across the country to go through the training class. We were not permitted to go home on the weekends, so I was away from Lisa for three straight weeks. It was tough, but I loved every second of it. I was like a kid in a candy shop, taking in everything my new job had to offer.

I was learning so much.

About science.

Sales.

Myself.

I always knew I wanted a job where I could throw my whole self into it, and this job finally confirmed it for me. I felt validated and affirmed. My "throwing away" of decent and stable opportunities wasn't ridiculous. It was strategic. I'd made it to where I envisioned myself for years.

As the weeks went on, I was, little by little, erasing my fear about sales and building my own confidence. This was something I could do. The training was thorough. We had time to practice and ask questions.

There I sat in training class, not employed as a sales professional for more than two months, and I could not help but be in complete awe of my instructors and trainers.

They knew exactly how to encourage, energize, and ignite desire in their people. There was a passion for both role and product that I'd never seen before. They took their time and made sure everyone in the room understood what was being asked of them.

And I . . .

I wanted *their* job.

I could do *their* job.

I had a biology degree, and I was a teacher.

But *they* were also salespeople before this too.

I needed to prove myself in the field of battle before I could take on one of these high-profile gigs.

I couldn't put the proverbial cart before the proverbial horse.

The corporate office was in Connecticut. I had never spent much time there. People who are not from the East Coast consider Pennsylvania to be ranked among the jumble of states that all collide around the Atlantic coastline. It's true that Pennsylvania is a hop and skip from New York, New Jersey, Washington, DC, etc. But *Erie*, Pennsylvania, might as well be a world away from the I-95 routes around Philadelphia. We were as far away from the state hopping as one could be, so I wasn't too familiar with Connecticut at all. But Lisa was.

Born and raised in Boston, New England as a whole was her home. She hopped and skipped with the best of them. My Connecticut-based training class was happening right after Thanksgiving, and Lisa had not been home in a while. I told her that I would go to Boston for Thanksgiving and then drive down to Connecticut for training because why not?

This was a big deal.

She was shocked.

I had *never* missed Thanksgiving with my parents in twenty-five years.

But I would, for her.

Lisa.

Plus, I had never met her family except for her mom. Her mom had come out to Erie to investigate this truck driver dating her daughter, and I had passed the "test" with flying colors. Lisa's family had connections in Erie, so staying in Pennsylvania for the holidays hadn't been so crazy. When her mom came out to visit and meet me, we took off for a local ski resort to catch the peak of the fall foliage. The leaves were deepening in color, my love was deepening for Lisa, and we had officially received the maternal stamp of approval.

This particular Thanksgiving would be the first of many trips to Boston for the holiday, and her family could not have been more different than mine.

They were short in stature and low in numbers. My family holiday gatherings hovered around forty-plus people, while theirs would top out at twelve. My family often has to duck through doorways to not hit our heads. Lisa's family did not have this problem. But height and numbers aside, there was a comfortable feeling with her family, one that I wanted to hold onto and make permanent in due time.

By the time training was done, the Christmas holidays were upon us, and there was not much time to get out in the field. My boss gave directions to "get a plan together," routing schedules, contact lists, etc. I took the time, organized, and was fired up to get out there and make a difference.

The last months and weeks of the year were . . . interesting.

It was 1999.

The Matrix was in theaters, *The Sopranos* premiered, Slim Shady came in second to Britney, and, depending on who you talked to, the world was going to end.

Tech people were convinced that computers were going to stop working on December 31 because the all-knowing technology would not know how to roll over to the year 2000. People were freaking out. Governments and private industries spent millions of dollars trying to avert the pending doom. Fear took over. Banking was sure to collapse. And the world would follow.

Y2K.

What a time.

At the end of the day, nothing happened. Australia was the largest country to ring in the new year, and civilization did not collapse.

I treated the new century as a new beginning for myself and Lisa. Even though I had only been employed in the health care field for two months at that point, I finally felt like I was focused.

I had found my purpose.

I truly believed in what I was doing.

I felt challenged and ready to grow.

I also learned that I loved watching and helping my brother start and grow his business. Witnessing his entrepreneurial spirit, passion, and drive piqued my level of curiosity on what I could do. Even though I was newly hired and hadn't yet sold a thing, my mind was looking for the *next* thing. But I needed to execute what was in front of me first before that next step would happen.

I never bought into the Y2K concerns because, quite frankly, I could not do anything to avert it myself. I could only control what I could control. I was ready to walk away from the nineties and into the twenty-first century with unbridled enthusiasm.

Prince wanted us to party like it was 1999, so I did.

My final lesson of the twentieth century?

Don't drink an entire bottle of champagne on your own.

The clarity I was seeking in the new year was slowed down by one of the worst hangovers of my life—or, at least, at that point in my life. But change, in the best way, was coming.

I could feel it.

The first full week of January 2000 was on. The two months of training and field preparation were over.

I had my plan, routing schedule, and all my sales materials ready to go. My confidence was running high. Dressed in my suit and tie, this time I was a pharmaceutical sales professional and not an office supply rep. This felt like me. It felt like home. I was ready.

I stepped out into the cold January air, started my car, and started rolling hot to my first call of the day.

My first call as a sales *professional*.

Given that I lived outside of my territory, I always had a drive of at least forty-five minutes. This was perfect. I had my Rand McNally physical map to get me where I needed to go. I was heading to Oil City, Pennsylvania. The windshield time gave me the opportunity to get my head straight and do a little pregame pep talk on what I was going to accomplish for the day.

Since this was going to be my first call ever, I was pretty jacked up. I rehearsed how I was going to introduce myself and ran the questions through my head that I was going to ask the doctor and nurses.

As I got off the highway and started snaking my way through the back roads to Oil City, I started to feel a little anxiety building up. Attempts to shake it off were not working.

With each mile marker, I was getting closer to my new reality, my new career.

That which I worked so hard to achieve.

I kept reminding myself that I had just completed training, and I killed it.

I knew my materials.

I verbalized everything.

I had my routing schedule.

Everything was in order.

I was ready.

. . . But I wasn't.

I had never spent any time in Oil City, so I did not know what I was getting into. But, nestled in between rolling hills, streams, and rivers, the ride was absolutely beautiful. I was trying to distract myself with what I was looking at.

As I made the last turn, I got a glimpse of the historic city. It had seen better days, but the buildings contrasted beautifully against the natural setting. Unfortunately, the vista did nothing to squelch the now-raging anxiety.

I looked at my routing list, and the doctor's office was in a historic office building on Main Street. I could see it. It wasn't more than one mile from where I was. But there were far too many stoplights for this small town, and each stoplight was programmed to turn red just as I went through the one before.

Of course.

As I inched through town, I could feel my anxiety building at each light. I hit the last light, and the doctor's office was halfway up the block.

I pressed the gas pedal.

I went through the light.

At this point, I was in a staring contest with the building.

I was locked in; the first call of my professional career was about to go down, and my heart rate was not letting me forget it.

Nope.

Not that day.

The pressure was too much.

The fear of failure too real.

This wasn't the job I thought it was going to be.

I broke off from my staring contest with the building and just kept driving.

I was alone, embarrassed, and ashamed. I followed the road right out of town and back on the highway toward home. The last few months of training and preparation were all for nothing. There were too many unknowns, and I was not ready to risk it all. This was going to be way too much of a job for me.

It was 9:45 a.m. I made the forty-five-minute ride back to Erie. But there was one problem (among many I was sure to face from playing hooky on my first day)—I was still living with my parents. They would clearly question what the hell I was doing at home. That was not an option.

That damn *Kaveney Work Ethic*.

Lisa and I were in a solid relationship by that point, so I had a key to her apartment. I made it to her place, laid on the couch with my suit on, and turned on the TV.

Countless thoughts were running through my head.

Where would I go next?

What would I do if this job wasn't for me?

Why couldn't I just get out of the car?

I lost track of time and paid no attention to Lisa's apartment door opening. It was 12:30 p.m., and she was home for lunch. I can still picture her face.

"Jim! What is going on? Shouldn't you be in the field working?"

Sitting on the edge of the couch, I told her the whole story and how I needed to do something else. This was not going to be the job for me.

I can't remember the exact words she said to me, but it was a taste of tough love.

Man up, this is day one.

Call your boss, tell him what's going on, and get back out there.

You can't just sit here and hide.

Ouch.

But she, as usual, was right. I left a voicemail for my boss, John. He was the best. When he called me back, I told him that I did not think sales was for me. My mind was too flooded by memories of office supplies past, and my heart couldn't take another round of failure.

"Don't worry about selling!" he told me.

Wow.

I never would have guessed that it would be an option to be in sales and *not* worry about selling. Those were the most refreshing and anxiety-minimizing words I heard all day.

He ran me through a quick checklist that included a car, suitcase, clothes, routing schedule, and a map.

"Pack your bags and take a road trip for the next couple of days around your territory and don't worry about selling. Just introduce yourself, leave a business card, and see where things go. No pressure and call me in a few days when you get back."

Done and done.

That seemed like a nice plan and the direction I needed.

Over the next couple of days, I drove hundreds of miles, making my way through a few good-sized towns, but mostly small rural communities.

It was beautiful.

The people were kind and welcoming.

They had not had a sales rep with my therapeutics in a long time. They weren't laying out rose petals at my feet, but the welcome reception was awesome just about everywhere.

It was exactly the boost I needed.

I had put such unreasonable pressure on myself to perform on my first call that I scared myself out of it. I was so focused on what I thought the *result* of the call should be that I skipped over the process. I once again had flashbacks of money and turnover and "don't take 'no soliciting' signs as a 'no'" from my office supplies days.

But this was not that.

My boss gave me the opportunity to just be me—be social, listen, learn, and look to solve problems if possible. Success was going to come, but I really couldn't be in this ALONE! I needed a team around me, and my boss John was the start.

Part
two

CHAPTER 7

Leaving Hotel California

I spent the next few years growing in my profession, trying to be the best I could be. There were some wins and some losses, but generally, this sales career was infinitely better than the last.

I grew my sales territory to always be in the top 25 percent of the territory and the top 50 percent in the region for the entire time I was in the field.

More than respectable.

Commendable, some might even say.

But somehow, I also seemed to miss out on being the *number one* territory. This drove me nuts, and it drove me to work harder.

I started to take on greater responsibility in the district and ultimately became the district trainer and then one of the regional trainers. Through this new role, I was able to help all the new hires through their own learning journey and new hire training. This was a perfect blend of my newfound appreciation and talents in sales and my biology education. I was a salesman *and* a science man. A beautiful marriage of two seemingly disparate paths.

Additionally, this responsibility gave me the opportunity to meet more influential people within my company and continue to reassure my mentor, Laura, that I was doing what she expected me to do: succeed.

After about nine months in my new role as regional trainer, my boss's boss decided to ride with me. This wasn't entirely out of the blue, as I had worked to make a name for myself in the region. I made sure to work above and beyond the expectations of the role by bringing the new hires to Philadelphia days before their three-week "boot camp" at the national training center. The other regional trainer and I wanted to ensure that *our* people felt as comfortable and prepared as possible when they walked into rooms for presentations. This set our people apart, which ultimately trickled back up the ladder to my own preparedness.

After the day in the field with him, my boss's boss told me he was going to put my name in the ring for one of the national sales training vacancies in Connecticut. I just needed to give him my permission.

It would be an eighteen-month rotation and would get me set up to become a district sales manager. Beyond excited, I told him unequivocally yes.

Now, I did this without talking to Lisa first.

But for good reason.

It was 2003, and Lisa and I had been together for over three years.

Oh, and we got married within those years.

After one year of dating and nine months of engagement, we got married in July 2001.

Marriage wasn't just for sales and science; it was also, absolutely, for us.

During our time together, we had made several big trips out to Boston to see her family for one holiday or another.

Almost without fail on each of those trips, within an hour of our nine-hour journey back to Erie, I would hear her sweet voice next to me.

"Do you think we would ever move to New England?"

My response was usually something like, "It would be nice, but . . . both of our jobs, my massive family, and our friends all live in Erie. So, probably not!"

We would often joke that Erie was a bit like "Hotel California": you can check out any time you like, but you can never leave.

And that rang true for several years.

And it also rang true that a chance to move to Connecticut would have been met with a resounding *yes* from my wife.

So, the big boss left the ride-along with confirmation to submit my name. I stopped at the gas station to fuel up for the ride home and called Lisa to let her know.

Just as I expected, with just a few short words about the opportunity, she was on board.

The job wasn't a given, and the process would be rigorous, but it would be a start. Within a few weeks, my boss prepared me for the intense panel-style interview process.

I wasn't too nervous at the initial prospect. I mean, I had spent years on the job market perfecting my interview skills.

But this time would be very different.

I had never experienced anything like it. In my mind, the interview process was all about being able to teach scientific and sales content. But the interview wasn't about the sales training role. That part was already proven when I was a field trainer. They knew my sales ability.

This was an interview about the *next* job. Could I be trusted to lead a team of salespeople? Just because I was good at sales and good at training others in sales did not guarantee that I would be good at *managing* salespeople.

During the interview, I held my own and read the room, but could not quite figure out the body language of my interviewers.

It was all over the place.

My heart was pounding, sweat dripping down my chest under my suit-coat, and my mind was trying to formulate the correct (but honest) answers, all while assessing if I was sinking or swimming.

I left confidently, only to find out that I did OK, but not great.

I would need another twelve months of development before they would interview me again.

I was disappointed by the news but also comforted.

Maybe I wasn't ready for it. I believed everything happens for a reason, and the meaning behind this would surely be revealed at some point.

My boss and I worked on a plan, and I settled into my development for the next twelve months. I spent more time on ride-alongs with my peers. More time understanding what it means to be a manager. More time with opportunities to sharpen my leadership skills. And most importantly, to *train* in all aspects.

Just as fast as the summers move in Erie, so did my experience development. I barely made it through four months of preparation when my boss received a call from the corporate office.

It was August.

They needed me to join the team.

No further interviews or development needed.

They needed me right away.

I took two weeks to wrap up my affairs as a sales professional, turn the keys of my territory over to the next rep, and start climbing the corporate ladder.

I was never told why they needed me, but I did not care, and neither did Lisa.

We were moving to New England.

The whole move and opportunity felt right. Within a couple weeks of my new role, I was thrown into one of the largest training sessions ever. It was expected that I could handle and facilitate a training room for one of the most anticipated product launches in our company's history.

I walked into the empty ballroom and started counting the number of chairs.

Two hundred fifty.

The doors opened, and, like moths to a flame, the masses started filling up the seats.

My heart skipped a beat.

The microphone was on.

It was go time.

The feeling was incredible. I was full of boundless energy as I fed off the vibe in the room. Four hours came and went without a hitch. Just as the last person left the room, so did my energy and stamina. I was beat. It felt like I had just finished multiple 2,000-meter rowing erg tests.

"Four months ago, you struggled to get through the interview process and now you are commanding a room of two hundred fifty people, great work."

This came from a VP who had interviewed me; he watched me for the full four hours of training. I had no idea he was in the room, but it didn't matter. I did things my way, and it worked.

This was it.

I finally found what I was meant to do.

I had known for a while that my heart was in pharmaceuticals. But I was even *more* sure that my heart was in *leading* people within pharmaceuticals. Managing people. Leading people. Coaching people. Training people.

If I wasn't a six-foot-something professional in a suit, I would have jumped for joy.

I had so much energy and enthusiasm that I felt like I was levitating over the room—no magic tricks needed.

Within a few weeks of being in the department, I was no longer the newbie. The older trainers were assigned to their managerial rotations and shipped out, and the new training managers brought it.

This place seemed like a massive managerial production factory. I was one of eight training managers when I arrived, and that quickly turned into twelve.

I watched my skills, competence, and confidence grow exponentially in the role.

I was *good* at what I did.

I quickly hit my one-year mark in the training department, and the questions started swirling about where I would be assigned a district manager position. I was excited about the opportunity to take on my own team, but it would also require Lisa and me to potentially move again.

One of the things people forget to tell you about climbing the corporate ladder is that sometimes it requires you to climb into your car with all your belongings and your loved ones and restart your life.

It's all "follow your dreams," but it's easier said than done when those dreams are crossing city and state borders.

We liked New England and did not want to go anywhere else, but Lisa had essentially given me the "where you lead, I will follow" green light, and I was giving that same green light to the company.

At the same time, I started contemplating sticking with training for a while. It was exhilarating, and I was always with people. I didn't have to be ALONE! in the job because there was always someone else to be responsible for.

To be validated in your ability to do something well is a feeling like no other. It's the trophy at the end of a race. The applause at the end of a show. The claps on the back after a presentation.

I was hopeful and wondered if I could finally feel settled and make a career of it.

But the answer to that question would come unexpectedly and not in my favor.

It was a Tuesday morning, scheduled to be no different than any other morning. I was up early and ready to get my day started.

My cell phone lit up.

And again.

And again.

I had fifteen missed calls. Four voicemails.

Shit.

I grabbed my phone and listened to the first voicemail.

"Shit is blowing up at the office with a major corporate announcement. Throw on a suit and get here ASAP."

Suit? We all leaned into corporate casual for our day-to-day attire. This had to be serious.

My mind was all over the place, and my heart followed along, jumping in anxiety and anticipation for what I could be walking into.

I made it to the office, ran up the stairs to the third floor, and found my peer-training colleagues huddled together. They started spewing out partial facts and theories.

"The company was sold to another larger pharma company."

What?

At this point, our bosses arrived and filled us in on the facts. There was going to be a live presentation given by our global leader in the corporate theater to reveal the full extent of the news.

Our bosses informed us that we needed to get over to the theater, sit in the front row, and prepare to run the microphone around the room for the Q&A. Our campus was huge, with multiple four-story office buildings and a large manufacturing facility. Thousands of people were employed in this town.

We were the first ones inside.

It was almost a year to the date that I had presented in front of two hundred fifty people at my first training session.

The energy *then* was palpable—you could live off it.

Not this day.

I watched the doors open to the theater, and the looks on people's faces as they trickled in said it all. The energy in the building—in the people—was flatlining, barely a pulse. A pin drop could have been heard in the silence and stress.

The executive team and our global CEO walked into the room, and if possible, the already established silence in the room grew quieter.

Tall and fashionably dressed in his euro-cut suit, the CEO welcomed the audience. The whole scene—his dress, words, and mannerisms—were exquisitely engineered to match his German accent. This was "big business," and everything had to be perfectly scripted to minimize disruption even though, to the employees, the sky was falling. The CEO got through the pleasantries and dove right into the details of the acquisition.

Except, he kept referring to the coming together of the two companies as an "alliance." He explained how the *allied* company would take over all the brands within our pharmaceutical portfolio, with the exception of the oncology compounds. Our company would shift to being a "specialty" pharmaceutical company and get rid of its primary care products, but still earn royalties within the *alliance*.

Our company would continue to exist within this *alliance* but not in the primary care marketplace.

This was . . . really big news.

And I don't think, to this day, I've heard the word *alliance* used so many times in one sitting.

Sitting in the audience were the heads of sales, marketing, compliance, legal, and manufacturing, as well as the respective team members from each department.

In essence, we would all be gone.

In between his German-accented announcement and the audience's silence, quiet sobbing could be heard and reddened, tearful faces of the so-called *alliance* could be seen.

This was clearly not going well.

Regardless, the show had to go on, and the message continued to get even more tone-deaf. Everyone in the room was either going to have a new employer, lose their job because of redundancy, or have to move to New Jersey to the new company's *allied* headquarters.

After twenty-five minutes, the presentation was done, and the Q&A session began. This is where I came into play. Two of my training peers and I had the mics and quickly sat in attention, waiting for the signal to run to a raised hand.

Crickets.

Absolute crickets.

No one was raising their hand.

Everyone was stunned to silence as the announcement marinated in the room.

Well, I figured, *why not me?*

I'm not sure why that urge came over me, but it did, and so did the trembling hands and the sweat dripping down my chest. At this point, I had only spent five years working for the company, which was a relatively long time, but I wasn't a second-generation anything with them. I liked the company and felt that I could be there till I retired, like my dad did for IBM for thirty years.

Lisa and I were settled in our lives.

And not the kind of settled where I felt like I was *settling*.

Life was finally running smoothly.

I was not going to let my job and this company go down without a fight. I was not going to just let the last five years disappear with a snap of their upper-management fingers.

One of the benefits of my employment was that they had paid for me to return to school for a master's degree in organizational leadership. In my classes, we reviewed countless case studies of leadership gone wrong. Their investment in my higher education was about to come back and bite them in the ass.

I was witnessing a train wreck in organizational leadership right before my eyes and was now equipped with the knowledge to recognize and call it out.

Carefully engineered, though, of course.

I waited a few more seconds to see if anyone else would raise their hand. No luck.

With my hands shaking, I put up one hand while death-gripping the microphone with the other. I was immediately called on. The exchange went like this:

Me: "I want to thank you for taking the time to explain to us that this is not an acquisition."

Him: "You're welcome."

Me: "However, I need a bit more clarity on the difference between the two words. Last year, we launched a drug with another pharmaceutical company as part of a co-promotion. We were, and are, *allies* in promoting the product. I am aligned with our company, and my peers-in-training from the other company are aligned with theirs. We get paid by our respective employers. That's a pretty straightforward example of an *alliance*. In this situation, would I be getting paid by our company or the new one?"

Him: "You will be paid by the new company."

Me: "Thank you. But if I am no longer getting paid by our company, then I don't really see how this isn't a classic case of an acquisition."

Gasp!

An immediate collective gasp was heard throughout the theater, and all the last remaining oxygen was sucked out.

It was the loudest silence ever.

And just like the sound of someone getting revived by CPR, the oxygen came back into the room and right into the CEO's now-aggravated lungs.

"It is . . . it is an *alliance!*"

There was that word again.

His tall frame towered over me from the stage. I had now officially disrupted the fine-tuned and corporate-engineered Q&A. I know I stayed through the rest of the discussion, but I really can't remember what happened from that point until I got back to my office on the other side of the campus.

I must have just blacked out or blocked out what was unfolding before me.

It wasn't even noon, and I was exhausted and spent. My office light was off, and the door was open. I sat down, took a deep breath, and noticed the voicemail light on my phone flashing rapidly.

In the span of the five minutes it took me to get to my office, my voice-mail was full of messages from people I knew—and a few that I didn't—thanking me for having the "balls" to ask the question everyone wanted to but didn't.

My chest puffed up.

I felt like a bit of a hero for speaking my mind and advocating for the majority.

I witnessed an organizational leadership catastrophe, and I wanted to right the wrong.

I felt vindicated for my actions.

It would not change things, but I could check the box for speaking up. I oversaw some of these people, and they needed to see me stand up for them.

In the afternoon, my peers and I met our bosses to learn the fate of our department. The manager-in-training program would be different under the new company.

In fact, we would have to interview for our jobs.

Damn it.

I wasn't worried as much as I was annoyed. They would be perceived as "rubber-stamp" interviews, as the *alliance* needed us to continue maintaining the training programs for each of the brands. We could also choose to do something different and interview for that opportunity or take a severance package and move on. It was a formality, but one that I thought I had moved beyond years prior.

At the end of what felt like the longest day ever, I looked at the phone. No flashing lights, no messages of thanks, therefore no more boost of hero-status energy to close out my day.

I checked my email one more time before shutting down and saw an email from my HR department with a one-word subject line.

Congratulations!

Intrigued, I opened my email.

Congratulations, Jim, on your five-year anniversary with the company. This is a true sign of our company's strength and longevity and your commitment to it. On behalf of the company, we would like you to select a gift commemorating this accomplishment. Cheers to many more.

I laughed at the irony, selected the Waterford crystal serving bowl as my prize, and went home.

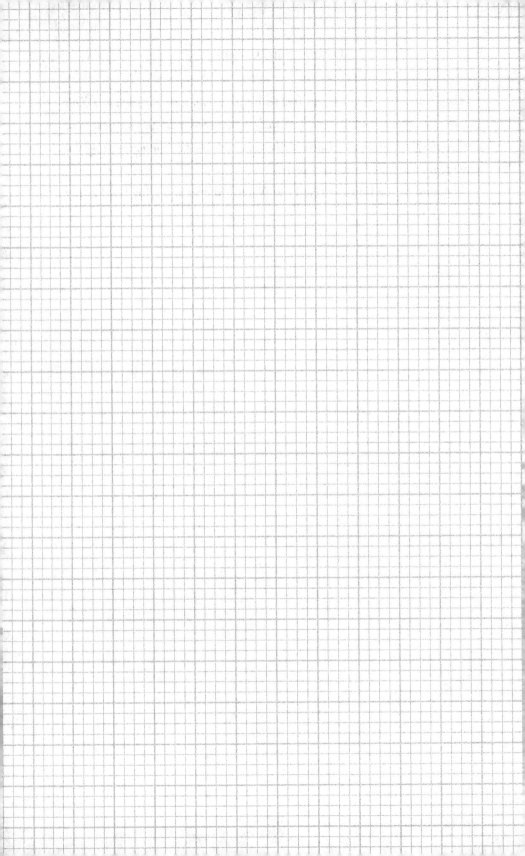

CHAPTER 8

Psychological Contract Crushed

osing my employer felt like I just got dumped.

My heart was somewhat broken, and my mind was all over the place.

Not knowing what was in store, I decided to let the process play out and see what was available.

One thing I knew for sure? We were *not* moving to New Jersey. We had settled in Connecticut and liked it. Besides, New Jersey did not have that "yeah, this feels right" feeling for us. And clearly, that feeling for me was the number one priority in decision-making. My work heart and marriage heart were in Connecticut. Garden State be damned.

But I would play along and not close the door just yet.

Within a little over a week, I met the man who would be my new boss, should I get "rubber-stamped" through the interview process. My reputation in the department was very good and I was seen as one of the leaders, not necessarily in title, but in practice. I was never much of a *titles* guy anyway, but I loved helping lead others.

The interview began.

"Jim, your reputation precedes you as being a leader and someone that is honest when giving feedback. So, with that, please tell me your opinion of how the rollout of the corporate news was delivered."

"*Really?*"

I was cautious. And optimistic. Seeking constructive feedback was definitely a green flag for our new employer. The train wreck I'd seen a week earlier was starting to clear up.

"Yes, really."

"OK, if you want my *honest* opinion, here goes. I get it. I get that uncomfortable business decisions have to be made in order for an organization to survive, etc. But the way it was rolled out was less than ideal. I just spent the last few years working on my master's degree in organizational leadership, where we analyzed case studies on what *not* to do. What was even more ironic about my degree is that my thesis was all about psychological contracts and the impact they have on employee–employer relationships. And my research was done within *this* company.

"Simply put, a psychological contract refers to the unwritten, intangible agreement between the employee and employer and the commitments within their relationship. This is different from the legal employment contract that everyone gets when obtaining a job: the employee provides labor to the company, and the company, in turn, provides compensation. The psychological contract is more informal and based on the perceptions of what each side of the agreement is. For example, job security, opportunities for growth and development, the employer's reputation, and a supportive boss. The list could go on, but the influence of the psychological contract on an organization can be huge.

"With that in mind, this is how I saw it: A good portion of the people in the audience were generational employees; the others were just long-standing, dedicated, American employees. Both were learning that their careers were about to be flipped upside down, if not outright eliminated, here in America. The job security they perceived to have was gone. But, following that devastating news, they get four or five slides about how beneficial this was going to be for the company in Japan. With all due respect, I am not Japanese, nor am I moving to Japan. So what's the point of rubbing that into the American employees' faces?"

He sat there expressionless.

Which was not so different from the way he looked at the beginning of the interview.

So, I thought nothing of it.

Oops.

The interview ended with an agreement to connect soon. I took no more than five minutes to get back to my office, but by the time I got over there and settled in, there was a knock on my office door.

Everything always seems to happen in those five minutes of getting back to my office.

The knock on the door was my boss.

She wanted to discuss how the interview went. She had something to share.

"Jim, the interview did not go well."

What?

"We just talked for a while and were open and honest," I told her.

Well, that was the problem.

By the time I left the interview and got to my office, a phone call was made. Based upon my honest answer to his *trick* question, I was deemed angry and hostile to the corporate change.

My quick psychological contract with this man was crushed.

No opportunities were going to await me in New Jersey. Turnpike and Shore be damned. I had to proceed with a severance package and start looking for another opportunity.

I took a few deep breaths as I processed this news.

It wasn't the end of the world. I was actually excited to see what else was out there.

Ghosts of the world being my oyster started to swirl around me.

But I was also pissed.

Why ask for my honest opinion if they did not actually want it? The whole notion of "say what you mean and mean what you say" was shot. Their *alliance* bullshit was nothing more than a Band-Aid on an amputation.

Clearly, I was not cut out for this corporate game. Or maybe the interviewer was just not aware of the importance of a psychological contract.

Out of twelve of us trainers, ten continued with the new company and two of us would go on what was one of the greatest end-credits training road trips ever.

We spent four weeks flying around the country, training all the new company's executives and field leaders on the products. We knew we were out of a job and had nothing to fear in that eleventh hour on our way out the door.

It was exhilarating. We killed it and found members of the new company asking us to reconsider the severance and join the team.

Those were validating requests, but my mind was made up. The damage of the trick interview was done. I'd mentally and emotionally moved forward. A whole new chapter was about to begin.

CHAPTER 9

New Chapter

My era in training experience went on hold.

In my mind, I was well qualified to be back in the job market. I was a successful sales rep and trainer and was just shy of becoming a manager. These were solid credentials, and finding an opportunity should have been a breeze.

Oh, how wrong I was.

First, the one large pharmaceutical company in Connecticut just laid me off in the name of an *alliance*. The other big companies were in places we did not want to be (*cough cough*, New Jersey). Therefore, training was out of the question for the time being.

Second, one company's perception of me being ready for a managerial role certainly did *not* qualify me for any leadership positions. They were looking for managerial experience, *not* almost-made-it-to-being-a-manager experience.

I realized the chances of having to return to sales were high. But after moving up into the national training manager role and taking on a significant amount of responsibility, returning to sales seemed like a huge step backward. In fact, the idea of it turned my stomach.

My heart was not interested in diving into the sales rep interview process, but my mind was telling me otherwise because, you know, money.

But wait!

I had severance for three months!

Maybe something better would come along if I just held out!

Severance existed for a reason, right?

Then, the reality of living in one of the most expensive states in the country blasted me back into the cold truth as quickly as I came out. Lisa and I needed dual incomes to survive and, ideally, to thrive.

So, fine. Job market it was.

Interview after interview, but nothing piqued my excitement. The fear of potentially having to return to printer paper and cartridge ink started to haunt me.

Not to mention that we were nearing the end of the year, which meant no openings till the start of the new quarter. When the ground starts to freeze, most major companies go into a hiring freeze because of end-of-year numbers, taxes, reports, etc. I got it, but I hated it.

Then, my sister Suzanne's friend Tony came through for me. He worked for another decent-sized pharma company that was looking for an oncology sales rep in Connecticut.

For pharmaceutical sales reps, getting into oncology sales was the holy grail.

The cream of the crop.

The best of the best.

Once you were in, you were set for a long time.

If you performed, of course.

The interview process could not have gone better. I connected exceptionally well with the manager. They were looking for a unique skillset because the supposed cream of the crop wasn't cutting it in the Connecticut territory. They needed to hire someone who knew sales, was good at sales, and didn't have the entitled "I am an oncology sales rep" attitude.

They needed a worker; a grinder who was used to putting in hours to get the job done.

Ah, the blessed and beautiful *Kaveney Work Ethic.*

The last leg of the interview process was to do a ride-along with Tony, the golden boy of the district. Apparently, he'd won Rep of the Year multiple times and was legitimately the cream of the crop. I was nervous and intimidated even before I met him.

The ride-along took place in Boston. I was going to see what it was like to call on one of the biggest and best cancer centers in the world. It turned out that that was the most intimidating part of the day.

This guy was nothing like I thought in the best way possible.

It was a Friday. We finished our calls around 3:00 p.m. He took me to a bar to do our field ride debrief. I assumed it was to grab a quick bite but was immediately corrected.

"Let's just grab a couple of beers and talk shop," he said.

Wait a minute.

It had to be a test. Another trick question by a company to weed me out of the running. If I said yes to a drink, I'd be deemed a . . . different . . . sort of liability. I'd been burned once, and even though the smell of hops was enticing after a long day, I wasn't going to be tricked. I hesitated and he noticed.

"Oh, the job is yours. I like you and think we need someone like you. I will recommend to Bob, our new manager, that you are the one."

Aw, shucks.

Screw the trickery.

A round of beer was ordered.

Cheers to the cream of the crop.

Excited (and more importantly, relieved) by what I could see was a transparent, good dude, I threw back a couple of beers with my lunch.

Lisa and I were spending that weekend in Boston at her parents' house, so I quickly drove to their place to let her know how well it went. Standing with her parents, I told her all the details and how excited I was. She had not seen this level of energy in me for any other opportunity since I was laid off.

"Oh, by the way, Tony was a cool dude, and we even had a few beers over lunch."

"You did *what*? Are you crazy—it was a test!"

My heart sank, and my mind started rushing again with all the negative outcomes of my decision.

Shit. Maybe it was a test. Maybe it wasn't going to happen.

A week later, my fears were put to bed. It did work out. The formal offer came through, and within just a few weeks, my new role in oncology sales began.

The new-hire home study process was intense. This was *oncology*. A whole new playing field and the complexity of the disease states were fascinating. The training to get us out on the street was rigorous.

Thankfully, my biology degree laid yet another solid foundation for me to build off of, but we were going deep into molecular and cellular components of the body. This was definitely the big leagues.

The home study process took four months and was followed by a couple of weeks of training in Seattle. Given my experience as a trainer, I was ready to critique the training managers who were training me. I'd dealt with a lot of good and bad trainers over the years, so I put my assessment hat on, and . . .

They were incredible.

Gifted.

They knew the disease states forward and backward.

Damn.

If I wanted to get back to that role, I was going to have to put in some serious learning time. The big leagues, indeed.

For as much as I was trained, the harsh reality of engaging with oncologists was beyond what I was prepared for. There was no easy, straightforward discussion. The complex nature of the disease, plus the labyrinth of treatment options, treatment complications, and patient outcomes, was overwhelming.

I could barely last a few minutes with a doctor before I would have to say, "Hold up, you lost me there."

I left training competent in the material but not proficient. It took many more months to get there. As scary as the first year was, I felt like I had purpose. This was the place where I wanted to be. I needed to perform.

My new company was incredible. I found my leadership team to be transparent, supportive, sincere, and real. This was the complete antithesis of what I experienced in the final days of my last job.

This was a *welcome* change.

This felt like home to me.

My first year of selling was a bit bumpy, but the expectations were, thankfully, low.

The New Year–kickoff sales meeting announced the winners from the year before. The golden boy Tony won yet again. I told him I was coming after him, but I just wasn't sure I could catch him.

In that same meeting, they also announced where the sales winners of the year would go for the award trip and announced the location for the upcoming year's winners.

Portugal.

The sales team erupted, the friendly chatter and competition already beginning. I told myself Portugal wasn't for me. It was going to be a tough year. I had already made up my mind.

I did not think I could make a difference.

I just did not think I could overcome how deep in the red the territory was when I took it over.

I had spent only eight months in the territory at that point.

I spent time figuring out my routing schedule, where I was going, where my access was, and what my message was.

I . . . needed a new mantra!

I was beyond the cold anxiety of making the first sales call to new doctors. I had been to each account but, in most cases, had not had the chance to talk to everyone. So, I did exactly what my first boss said to do.

I went out and introduced myself.

Most importantly?

I did not *sell.*

I wanted to establish a level of trust and understanding. I wanted to do a great job this year and show everyone that I could take on oncology and win. I was going to focus only on the *process* and enjoy the hunt. My mind was locked in.

Doors that had been closed for years suddenly opened. Innovative approaches to selling and engaging were making a difference.

By the end of the third quarter, I was actually in the running for the Portugal trip.

Portugal.

I was number one in the district and in the top ten nationally.

Portugal.

Shit. It was a close race. And I wanted to win.

I did not want this realization to become a distraction, so I tried (and struggled) to keep it out of my mind. At the end of the day, I did it.

Portugal.

I was on my way. I took down the golden boy and became Rep of the Year.

Boom.

I had taken on oncology and won.

A ten-day adventure with other coworkers and leaders within the oncology division. To put it lightly, it was a blast. It was something that, before, I never thought possible.

But as exciting as it was, *Portugal* was not the main cause for celebration. It was that I was once again doing something I loved and doing something that could truly save lives. Pharmaceuticals as a whole is no walk in the park, but we were helping people beat cancer. I didn't see anything other than blue skies.

My stint in oncology sales didn't last long.

My history in training was now finally being recognized, and they wanted me to take on a national training role.

In Seattle.

But I could still live in Connecticut!

. . . or on a plane.

Lisa and I transitioned for a while to a bicoastal marriage. She visited on the weekends when I had to be there for an extended period. If I had some flexibility, I would fly back to Connecticut for a week or so at a time. Sometimes we were able to even pull off two weeks here, two weeks there.

It worked.

We worked.

We did not have kids to worry about and were both working so hard to climb our respective ladders. Traveling for work was nothing new in my world, and this just felt like an extended version of what we had been doing all along.

Did we always like it?

No.

But in some ways, it brought us closer. We were both committed to each other and to our goals. We both knew that this was where we were *supposed* to be at the time. It was a great setup.

About six months into my training gig, I got a call from my mentor, Laura. This call was not unexpected. After she left our last company, she was blazing new trails across the industry. She could not provide many details, but she was working with some new people to launch a startup.

Interesting.

Allegedly, all the good money was in startups.

"Are you interested?"

Of course I was interested, but I was also happy. And I usually preferred how I *felt* to how much I made. And this felt a bit . . . risky. She let me know it was very much in the pilot stages, and she would not bring me in if it wasn't going to be something.

Deal.

I asked her to keep me posted.

Again, there she was, looking out for me.

People helping people.

I appreciated the phone call, but I was feeling good where I was. I was riding high and thinking that my leadership team had it right. I am sure there were organizational issues that I was not aware of, but my organizational-leadership-red-flag radar did not go off.

That is, not until one of the biggest face-palm/irony moments of my career.

New Chapter

Waking up in my permanent hotel room in Seattle after one of the many cross-country flights, I got a phone call from my training partner.

No "hello."

No "good morning."

Just "I hope you liked working at your prior company because they just bought us."

No.

Just a few years ago, I was being screamed at by an extremely tall boss-man about the benefits of downsizing, *alliance*, and focusing on the smaller oncology business unit. Now, they were buying a very large—not huge, but large—pharmaceutical company that was the global leader in women's health care, *primary care*, not oncology. My former company was going back into primary care after firing everyone in Connecticut and shipping off their products to another firm.

Apparently, the business benefits in Japan were not paying off.

Within a few months of the announcement, my boss in Seattle left the department, and a new manager was brought in.

He was based in . . . New Jersey.

The new company was shutting down the Seattle office and moving everything to New Jersey, training included. There would be no remote working conditions. They gave me three months to start looking for housing in New Jersey, and, in the meantime, I would have to live in a hotel five days a week, with no flexibility to come down the Turnpike every other week.

Lisa and I were on the same page.

There was *still* no way we were moving to New Jersey.

More importantly, going back to work for the company that laid me off just did not sit well with me. Again, I understand business. But, watching this company reverse a decision they had made just a few years before, with such collateral damage and job loss, seemed shitty at best and a colossal disaster at worst.

Lisa was also thriving in her job; she had climbed to the rank of chief operating officer, which is not a small feat. She was running the show at work, and I was not about to drag her away from that.

We played the game, of course, and looked at houses, but we had no intention of making the leap into New Jersey. We said no before, and we were saying it again.

This move was *not* going to happen.

CHAPTER 10

Start It Up

A pattern emerged in my job search.

If I were a training manager, I could never find a job in training. Since beggars can't be choosers, I took a sales job with a different oncology company. I tried not to think of it as a step back but rather as a calculated choice to get closer to what I wanted. I was not going to feel like another victim of corporate circumstances if I could help it.

This time, the new company was a startup. This was a tough job to get, and I went through eight interviews before getting the offer. The last interview was with the head of sales and marketing. She was a friend of Laura.

People helping people.

I left behind another train wreck in leadership, and I was hoping this time would be different.

This was my first experience in a startup.

I received stock options and was, technically, a co-owner of the company.

The entrepreneurial spirit was alive and well.

We all bought into the mission and vision.

The leadership was great.

The culture was great.

Unfortunately, the product was not.

All pharmaceutical companies live and die by the decisions of the Food and Drug Administration (FDA). They either approve or deny the marketing of any drug or device. This is based on the data and research conducted by the company. The company bears the responsibility to do the right thing and do their due diligence before submitting a product into the world, but the final decision rests with the FDA.

Because I was technically an owner, I took even more interest in the behind-the-scenes activity with the FDA. My focus veered toward how the process works rather than just trying to sell the end stage of that process. My company's meeting with the FDA was scheduled, and the hearing and decision rendered could be listened to via conference call.

The call was scheduled for 3:30 p.m.

I listened intently to the discussion. The exchange back and forth with the FDA and my company's representatives was fascinating.

At the end of the day, our scientists had to act like salespeople. They needed to tell a convincing story.

They didn't.

And the data didn't either.

At the beginning of the call, I excitedly sat up with the perfect posture of a kid who had gone through years of altar server training.

No slouching.

Ever.

As the call progressed and the story started to fall apart, my spine collapsed into the chair and my hopes collapsed into anxiety.

Each side concluded their discussion. It was time to vote.

One by one, the nay votes came in from the panel of thirteen doctors, and after each vote, I slid lower and lower into the chair. The floor could have swallowed me alive, and I wouldn't have noticed.

It was over.

The job lasted eight weeks. Most of us were laid off almost immediately. We had only two months of employment under our belts, and yet they still gave us all five months of severance.

It was above and beyond.

I guess the startup money came in handy at the end.

And I began the process all over again.

My bootstraps were starting to fray from all the times I had to keep pulling myself up.

Things were starting to get pretty crazy in the world. The subprime mortgage fiasco of 2008 blew up and took the economy with it. We were going into one of the worst recessions since the 1930s.

It was no Y2K and the world was not ending, but a lot of opportunities were disappearing before they were even advertised.

The job search during this time was . . . difficult.

But after many months, I found yet another sales job in oncology. Fun company, great culture, and great products. The company would ultimately have one of those rare, positive meetings with the FDA for its drug and go on to launch one of the most successful oncology products at the time.

I didn't stay long enough to experience that.

I had only been with this company for a few months, but I was bored.

I could not do it.

I was calling on the same doctors and nurses as before.

I pretty much had the same exact territory.

There was no forward momentum.

The words "privileged" or "ridiculous" might start ringing in the ears again, but I had been on and off the job market enough at this point to know that if my heart wasn't in it, nothing else mattered. For better or for worse, I was convinced in my core that it was better to keep searching than to settle. And besides, why would a company even want someone who wasn't *all in*?

It was a cold, rainy, and raw Monday in Connecticut. I was tired.

Tired of the process.

Tired of the job.

Tired of the hamster wheel that was my career.

My exhaustion was interrupted by a phone call from Laura.

"Hey Jim! I told you I would keep you posted when things were ready. They are ready. How would you like to come and work for me to be a regional business director for the Northeast?"

Yes.

It was like a knife of sunshine had come slicing through the gray day.

"OK, great," she said. "I need you to get on a plane first thing tomorrow and fly to Orange County, California. Don't worry about your resume, just come and talk to my new boss and the CEO of the company. I put my name behind you. Just be yourself and the job is yours."

My proverbial oyster was looking westward where dreams *do* come true.

This was moving ridiculously fast.

Becoming a regional business director would be a massive step forward in my career.

I had to do it.

I immediately called Lisa and told her the news.

There was a brief amount of hesitation because it was a startup biotech company, and the risk was real. My success with startups was . . . not great at this point.

But it was backed by Laura.

I was backed by Laura.

And because of Laura, Lisa was on board.

We jumped at the chance.

Within twenty-four hours, I was on a plane to California. I arrived Tuesday, prepped for the interview Wednesday, caught the red-eye Wednesday night, and was back home Thursday.

I was still tired, but this time in a much more exhilarating way than at the beginning of the week.

The process was a breeze, and the job was ultimately mine.

The following week, I was in the Big Apple, New York City, hanging out at the swanky Yale Club and meeting the company's board of directors. I was floored. Literally one week prior, I was one of a hundred salespeople, now I was truly on the ground floor of a startup and helping shape the foundation of the company. I knew I worked hard to get here. The pile of resumes and applications I churned out over the years was testament to my efforts. But it still felt incredibly wild to me.

To have someone in your corner batting for you.

To have an opportunity like this in a job and market that ravaged people's lives in the early 2000s.

To feel, once again, like I had found my new home.

In the first ten months of the job, I drove 50,000 miles. The highway was my new best friend.

Unfortunately, the product we were selling was not sexy and had no advantage, clinically or financially, for patients or providers. It was a new version of a generic drug, so nothing special. My heart was 100 percent in this job; I just wished the product was 100 percent up to my enthusiasm.

Selling was hard.

Until it wasn't.

Things did not change because of any amazing sales approaches we tried. No matter how charming one could be to potential buyers, a branded generic was nothing more than a branded generic.

It was sheer luck that changed *everything*.

The company managed to capture lightning in a bottle. Due to manufacturing delays and a lack of incentive, the generic manufacturers stopped making the product, and there was a significant shortage.

And *we* had the only other option approved by the FDA and on the market.

Two things happened because of this shortage.

One, I witnessed how the company took a huge risk on a product to establish a commercial presence in the country. If the shortage didn't happen, we would have most likely been out of jobs within a couple of months.

I was grateful for that.

Grateful that the company was willing to take the risk and grateful to not be out of a job.

The company now had a significant windfall in cash and could further secure its finances, put away some money for a rainy day, and then go and buy another asset to further establish our commercial presence.

I loved being a part of the entrepreneurial game playing out.

The second thing I witnessed was the clear raising of a red flag.

Somehow, we all missed it.

But it was right there in front of us; in fact, it was a red Ferrari pulling out of each of our driveways. We were all salespeople, we loved competitions, and the CEO knew how to dangle a bright and shiny carrot in front of us.

At the time we launched the product, there was very little hope of making any real bonus money. But we all had just left our jobs, so Laura, in her thoughtful way, had offered us two options.

One option paid a guaranteed bonus for working our butts off, and then, if sales took off, we would get a smaller amount of money on the back end.

Option two, don't take any guaranteed bonus and go all in and have faith that the product will take off and you could make significant cash and stock options on the back end. Everyone took the guarantee.

But the CEO wanted to add a *kicker*, regardless of which option you chose.

If the company could bring in $13 million in revenue, he would personally buy each of us a Ferrari. No, this wasn't in writing, but it was spoken over and over again.

Talk about psychological contracts.

This was a very big red one.

When we weren't selling any product, I was grateful for the guarantee. But the shortage and ensuing skyrocket of success changed all of that.

We beat the revenue target by $500,000.

I killed it on the bonus, and I could smell the fresh Italian leather of my Ferrari already.

That dream was quickly dashed. Standing in front of the ten of us, the CEO proclaimed that none of us would get a Ferrari, regardless of hitting the number.

Why?

Because he said it had to be $13 million *net* revenue and not gross.

It certainly felt gross.

No, the promise of a Ferrari wasn't in writing, but to me, that wasn't the point.

I could see that the underlying nature of this man was founded upon greed. He didn't care about the promises made; he cared about the dollar signs. And this nature, over time, infected a few others in our group. The red flag drove off into the sunset without us, and we all looked away.

Maybe blinded by the opportunity.

Maybe hopeful that this time was an anomaly.

CHAPTER 11

Training Acceleration

Within a whirlwind new season for the company, we acquired another product. A *real* product with true clinical data. Actually, unbelievably, life-changing data.

But it was a complex product.

Relatively difficult to coordinate treatments for patients.

Oncologists . . . didn't want to use it.

It was too much hassle, and they had other options that were providing real benefit to patients too. We would be the third company to own it. It was up to us to reverse the course and breathe new life into it. We weren't going to be able to do that with just ten of us. We needed to build. Fast.

My regional business director title would now actually mean something. I was going to have a team of five sales reps reporting to me, and since we were a startup, I would continue to be the director of training and *also* take on the role of an assistant director of marketing.

I was busy again and getting rewarded for it.

I loved every minute of it.

We went out and hired the best of the best, all former President's Club winners who were in the top 10 percent of their respective sales teams. We were going to flip this thing around quickly.

During all of this, the original ten people would take on new roles and shift to other areas of the business. Laura was no longer the head of sales.

I had a new head of sales, Eric. The one and only. A good guy who liked to speak his mind. He trusted me and I trusted him. I reported to him for both sales and training.

I put together a shotgun training program to get the new team out and in the field. It was clunky, but it served its purpose. There was no time to waste.

We were going to ride these newfound successes forward.

But . . . that did not work. After an initial uptick in sales, the downward trend continued. Oncologists didn't have the time or patience to figure out this new drug, and we were moving so fast, most of the reps barely had time to wrap their own heads around the product.

Something needed to change if we wanted to ensure that this company would exist beyond the hype of the moment.

I needed to get out there, back in the field, to see what was happening on the ground level with the product. So, I flew to Nebraska on one of the coldest winter days I had ever experienced to meet the top doctors of that region's sales rep. She was the number one rep in the country, and I was looking forward to seeing the rumored excellence.

Unfortunately . . . I saw nothing of it.

She talked and talked and talked.

And talked some more.

Talked for ten minutes straight.

Never once did she ask the doctor a question.

She was showing off for me, but I didn't like what I was seeing.

I did not want to embarrass her, so I let her keep going. Looking down at my watch, I saw time was dragging, and neither I nor the doctor in question had time for this.

The doctor was politely letting this play out too, but I started to physically sweat. In the dead of winter. In Nebraska. She was missing so many chances to *engage*. I could feel the sweat soaking into my shirt and the reality of the situation soaking into my brain.

Thankfully, and miraculously, she paused to take a quick breath and get a drink of water. She slammed down the small cup of water and turned back to the doctor to start again.

Shit.

But the doctor jumped in and just told her to stop talking.

Politely.

He only had a few more minutes before he had to go back to his patients. This was it. The last shot. I decided to step in and engage him with a simple question.

"Why do you believe in the product you're using?"

He seemed taken aback.

"Why do you ask that question?"

I wanted him to tell me what particular value he saw in his product. Not that it was a bad product. Not a bad product at all. But I wanted him to defend his choice.

I wasn't trying to be combative. In fact, it was the exact opposite. I wanted to hear from this brilliant man what he believed to be so important about sticking with his current regimen for patients. He was data driven, so I wanted data to drive the conversation.

His response was both surprising and unsurprising.

His go-to treatment choice made him a hero.

When he switched over to his current treatment, he saw a 30 to 40 percent increase in response. Both he and his patients were emotionally attached. He got to save their lives. They got to live. It was a beautiful, symbiotic relationship.

Oh boy.

I knew this was going to be a tough sell.

I asked another question. This one, not so simple. I asked him if he could define the historical treatment landscape of the disease.

He was a doctor. Brilliant, but he couldn't be expected to remember every little thing.

"OK," I said. "I get it. You want high outcomes for your patients, and you're seeing that. But . . ."

I paused for dramatic effect.

"What if I told you that our product's data is showing just shy of an 88 percent response rate in patients?"

The "few minutes" he had left when the rep was talking turned into fifteen more.

During this time, I reviewed with him the *historical perspective of the management of the disease state.* It's a mouthful but crucial to patient treatment.

Everyone talks about keeping your eye on the prize, but when it comes to pharmaceuticals, I was learning that if you *only* look at the prize (patient response rates and sales), you are ignoring all the factors that directly influence that prize.

Historical context.

Drug advancement.

Disease progression.

Patient risk factors.

Our product had value. Value that, to this day, has yet to be matched.

But it was complicated. He knew it. And I knew it. But for a data-driven doctor who just wanted to save lives, I couldn't leave without breaking down for him how our drug fit into the historical perspective of management of this disease.

It was one of the most enlightening conversations both the rep and I had. Within a few days, that same doctor would treat three patients with our product. He just needed to be challenged a little.

And be asked a damn question or two.

I immediately called Eric with the answer to our company sales problems.

I had figured it out: we needed to change the whole way we were training our team. Simple, right? Burn everything down and start fresh.

Our teams had no idea how valuable a product we had on our hands. They didn't understand the history of the treatment of the disease, so they didn't understand why our option was worth selling. It was a *historical perspective of the management of the disease state* training (HPMDS).

Again, a mouthful. But a mouthful that would change the trajectory of my entire career.

I explained my idea to Eric, and he agreed.

"How fast can you get it up and running?"

"Three months."

"Do it."

I was put in charge of creating something from nothing.

I was reinventing the wheel.

I was ALONE! in this endeavor, but for the first time, it wasn't the worst thing.

We were still a startup, too young to invest in a team, and didn't have time to look elsewhere for support.

Eric gave me the green light, and I had to hit the ground running.

I only had one conversation with one doctor, but that one conversation led to a sale that led to an entire realization about how pharmaceutical training has failed everyone in the system.

When a product is launched, reps are trained on the benefits of that product and the positive treatment response, as well as that product's ranking amongst its competitors. All training provides a review of the disease state landscape, sure, but the main focus was on the in-the-moment benefits:

The data.

The numbers.

The efficacy.

The safety.

The sales.

The jargon.

It was an approach that allowed for a quick fix in product training but not one that sat well with doctors who did not have the time or patience to be talked *at*. I had seen it firsthand. I had witnessed my own salespeople operating in this way before I could step in and reset the process.

What the industry needed was a holistic approach to training, and I was the man in charge. I was pumped. Excited to take on the challenge of reviving a product that wasn't selling. My heart beat for this new idea. It was like I could see everything clearly for the first time in my career.

And let me just say:

I had never been so damn thankful for office supplies in my entire life.

I didn't think office supplies held any inherent, life-changing value. But I was proved wrong.

Binders became my new best friend. Binders and printing paper. And therefore . . . ink cartridges.

We had no budget for developing an entirely new training program, so I had to do everything the "old-school" way.

Binders and printing are considered "old school" now, but back then, it was the way to train. I copied and printed hundreds upon hundreds of research files, background reports, data analyses, etc., and compiled them all into binders. I needed to create a manual for how to study and discuss the history of a disease state, its treatment progressions, and how our drug fit into that holistic context.

It wasn't just a matter of "This product does X."

It was a matter of "This is when the disease was first diagnosed and treated. And over the years, we have learned X about the disease and tried X treatments. Today, with all of that knowledge, our company has developed X to continue the progression."

It was a lot.

And without those office supplies I walked away from in distain ten years prior, I could never have pulled it all together.

That and the *Kaveney Work Ethic*.

Three months move quickly when you are deep in the trenches of research and training development. I worked fast and probably harder than I ever had at that point in my career.

It was a fever dream of innovation.

And once it was all approved by upper management, we had to retrain the entire company.

I pulled together a team of the best reps in the country and we did a "train the trainer" trickle-down approach. I went into a deep dive with this select team of reps. We rolled up our sleeves, sat with the materials, and reviewed every single thing they needed to know about the HPMDS.

Historical Perspective of the Management of the Disease State.

We used all those blessed and beautiful office supplies to really get elbow-deep into our product.

Once this group was trained, we let them loose to train other reps. And once they were trained, they'd be let loose to implement the new strategy in calls with doctors.

I was 100 percent confident, and so was Eric.

But we also knew that this new strategy for training would not be for everyone. We told the reps that we would take a few months for an adjustment period. Let everyone get comfortable, try this method out, and see how it feels. If, for whatever reason, it wasn't clicking or they didn't feel like it was the right "fit" for them, we would help them find another job. Not in a threatening way, but in a genuine "we want everyone to be comfortable with this" kind of way. It would be hypocritical of me to be the man who goes with his heart but then tells his reps to do the opposite.

It was so much work for them. For me. But it was work that had to be done and once done, changed the culture of learning at the company permanently.

Sales of the product rose.

The confidence of the reps rose.

Admiration of the doctors rose.

My stocks rose.

I was officially an innovator.

I was hitting my stride both at work and home.

I . . . was pushing into my midthirties.

I wouldn't say that "father" time was calling, but being raised in a family of nine kids, I also couldn't deny the desire to expand our family.

We would be blessed with our first son in 2008 and our second in 2010.

Things changed for me when my boys arrived, as they should. My priority was to always put my wife first, but now with a full family, the decisions we made—the decisions I made—would have greater implications.

CHAPTER 12

Startup Infection

I can't say that the sales exploded overnight, but they did change course. Doctors told Eric and me that the engagement level improved, thoughtful dialogue was happening, and, in turn, behaviors were changing and patients were getting treated.

When I was hired, I was the youngest team member, both in years of age and with pharmaceutical experience. I trained and led sales professionals with twenty to twenty-five years of experience, but I was never intimidated. I wasn't going to change the way I thought was the right way to lead or train just because they'd been in the game longer.

Time and time again, I was told:

"I have been through a lot of training programs in my career, but none are as good as this."

"You have a talent, a gift."

"You should start your own training company."

For as many times as I heard it, I would dismiss it.

I loved training, but I knew nothing about starting a business, let alone a *training* one.

But these comments did pull out my desire to do something else on the side. I had always talked to Lisa about starting *something* of my own.

Funny enough, these somethings were never related to my field of expertise.

Why?

I don't know.

Maybe I was afraid of failing in my day-to-day profession, but I felt perfectly willing to jump off a bridge into a whole new world.

That idea was crazy.

Thus, I never acted on it.

The resistance was too strong.

But, from afar, I watched my brothers Brian and Tom transform their companies into huge successes. They loved their businesses and were killing it. They respectively loved painting, construction, and forging their own paths, and it showed.

Did I love anything so much that I could build a company?

I have always been a curious person. I look at the world and wonder if there is a better way to do something or a better way to build something. That level of curiosity started to build more and more throughout the years.

The company was growing wildly. It felt good to have the tenure that I did. We were making a name for ourselves, and the stock price was growing alongside the recognition. My hope for a startup windfall was in the making.

As we grew, new leadership came on board, which invariably created a ripple of changes and repositioning. I started to see people groveling for new positions and watched while the seed of greed that was seen early in my tenure started to take hold.

People wanted more power and authority.

More money.

They did not care who got in the way.

I witnessed long-standing friends turn on each other all in the hope of climbing one more rung of the corporate ladder.

I watched as Laura made personal sacrifices for the company, only to lose her job in the weirdest of ways. She had packed up her life on the East Coast and moved to California to meet the demands of the new leadership. It wasn't long after she unpacked her last box that management decided her role was "no longer needed." The person who was *actually* willing to go all in for the company, and for me, was left behind.

Things got ugly, fast.

The same individual who said he would step on anyone who got in his way . . . did.

He came after me.

I started getting blamed for situations that were not my fault.

Some of my people started questioning my level of commitment to the future of the company because it didn't *seem right* that I got to fly in and out of California whenever I wanted whereas they *had* to be there.

If something went awry in the marketing plan—even something that I had disagreed with originally but was outvoted on—I took the fallout.

My name was being dragged through the mud. Laura's "little project" wasn't really as good as she said.

Accusations of incompetence flew around quicker than I could cross the country to address them.

I was removed from meetings that I used to run with no explanation.

Eric did his best to navigate the stickiness of the situation, but he had his own job to do. I didn't blame him. I was just growing tired of being blamed.

My character was laid bare in front of the firing squad time after time.

But I kept on keeping on.

I did not need to justify anything to anyone.

I knew who I was. I did not know when, but I knew at some point I would be vindicated.

At that point, I had a family to think about. I could not make any rash decisions. I had to endure the shifting sands of leadership and hold tight.

While I was focused on my own issues, my boss was dealing with his own set of issues at the company, and once his outcome became clear, I knew it would be time to go.

I put my head down and executed my job and a plan for self-removal from what was turning out to be a legitimate leadership *shit show*.

Eric saw how I bounced back from the barrage of indictments and did my job at a high level. He told me repeatedly that I had a gift for compartmentalization. He was impressed with how I could put the shitty stuff aside and execute.

I did not know if it was a gift.

I was just doing what I always did and mentally pushing through, knowing it would take a lot of focus to push through *this* particular mess.

If I didn't push through . . . well, I had come so far from the intrusive thoughts of my childhood thinking of myself as a terrible person. I could not afford to go back to that place.

Even though my psychological contract with this place was shredded, my employment contract was still in play.

I had a good salary and a considerable amount of stock options.

I needed to position myself and my family in the best way.

What was that going to be?

It was my family. It was Christmas. Back in Erie with all of my siblings and their kids.

My oldest son was old enough to run around ragged with all his cousins, while my youngest was being passed from one person to the next. My brother's house was big, but forty people could fill up the space quickly.

The chaos brought me so much joy. It reminded me of growing up.

After a few days of holiday celebrations, we packed up the car and started the long drive back home to Connecticut. At this point, we had lived in Connecticut for eight years. We had a great network of friends, and Lisa's family was just a few hours away. Her side of the family was growing too.

Except they were still two hours away.

Nice, but not convenient. Her parents were semiretired and had moved to New Hampshire the summer before to be closer to Lisa's sisters and their growing families.

At first, I did not like the idea of moving to New Hampshire at all. Connecticut was my quintessential New England, and I loved it.

But on that particular trip home, I dropped a hint to Lisa that we should consider moving to New Hampshire so our kids could grow up around their cousins.

We both saw how much fun it had been in Erie.

I wanted my kids to have those same family-fun experiences that I did.

Just *not* in Erie.

There I was, suggesting we move *closer* to the in-laws, which was usually not my go-to.

That was a big suggestion for both of us.

For Lisa, it would mean a much bigger change than the home address.

She was doing great—better than great—in her career, but we had two kids and watched half our shared income go to daycare.

In my simple plan, we would move to New Hampshire and save money because it was much cheaper than Connecticut. In the "Live Free or Die" state, there aren't any income, sales, or capital gains taxes.

I would continue working for my company, and she would stay home with the kids. In theory, this was easy, but it meant that she would have to leave the company that she helped grow and take on the persona of being a stay-at-home mom.

This was easier said than done.

Lisa loved working.

The *Kaveney Work Ethic* was fiercely matched by Lisa's own stamina in the workplace.

But it was taking a toll. For better or for worse, I figured this move would be a breath of fresh air in the grind of our day-to-day existence.

I didn't want to control her or her career choices. The decision ultimately had to be a mutual one.

And it was.

I can't say that the extraction from her career was either easy or as difficult as an exorcism.

It was somewhere in between.

And it was all going to be OK.

I truly felt drawn—almost called to—New Hampshire. Once we chewed on the idea a little longer, it became the only vision where we could see ourselves.

I could sell some stock options to help pay for the new house and offset the loss of Lisa's salary. That spring, we started looking in every town. Her parents were *beyond* excited, and her mother eventually tipped us off to two houses for sale in their town on the same street. We missed out on the first one but got the second one.

It was done.

The real estate market at the time did not cooperate with us as we were coming out of the largest real estate collapse we had experienced.

The good news was we were able to buy an incredible newer home at a relatively reasonable price.

The bad news was we couldn't sell the home back in Connecticut.

We had to carry the pressure of two mortgages for a number of months. We stayed in Connecticut, and Lisa kept working throughout the summer until we were finally able to sell the house in the fall.

We were getting close to the holidays again and would be able to feel what it was like to wake up with her family nearby.

To us, that was worth the price of all the sacrifice.

As the calendar for the new year turned, things at my company turned for the worse. By that point, Eric was also under attack and his days were numbered.

This was it for me.

If he was gone, I could not stay for much longer.

For about a year, my mind was swirling with ideas of what to do. I was ready to jump into starting . . . something.

I was an innovator, for crying out loud.

I had a million and one ideas.

I spent countless hours of my life dreaming big.

How big?

I was going to launch a diaper bag company that was a little more "dad appealing."

I was a father of two boys—I knew the need and the gap in the market.

Drawings were made.

Website URL was purchased.

Logo was created.

Textile companies were researched for building a demo.

It was fun, but there was so much about this kind of space that I knew nothing about. I was learning, but there was still so much beyond my understanding.

Starting something from nothing *is* magic.

But it is also mayhem.

And while I enjoyed the mental thrill of a new chase, my heart wasn't in it.

And when my heart isn't in something . . . well, we all know how that goes by now.

It *had* to be training.

CHAPTER 13

The Courage to Jump

Throughout all our years of marriage, I had always shared the desire to build a business. Regardless of how many times I talked about it, the reality hadn't truly set in until after our first holiday in the new house.

"So, we moved to New Hampshire, I left my job to stay home with the kids, and now you are going to quit your job and we will have no income?"

Yup.

We had prepared for this. We had a few bucks in the bank, and we could live a bit tighter until it took off.

The *Kaveney Work Ethic* went nicely together with *Kaveney tight budgets.*

We could make it work!

I was sure of it!

She . . . thought I'd lost my mind.

We were only a few months into our new structure of life. Lisa was still adjusting to the shift from full-time working mom to full-time stay-at-home mom. I was throwing out every random entrepreneurial idea that popped into my mind.

But this time was different.

I was going to start a training company and quit my job and make it work.

I had to make it work.

For my own sense of self. For our family. For our future.

Sure, we wouldn't have health insurance or a 401(k) or vacations for a while, but it *felt* right.

Lisa didn't exactly hop on board at the drop of a hat, but I sure painted a nice picture.

A home office right around the corner from the kitchen.

I could wake up early every morning and grind out a few hours of work before the kids woke up. We could have breakfast together. And have afternoon cookies and milk together. And always be home for dinner. And help when she needed.

Norman *f*cking* Rockwell.

Pure idealism. Romanticism at its finest.

I had to make it work.

I did not know when it was going to happen, but I knew it was coming quickly.

I had to continue to crush it at work so as to not show any signs of slowing down.

There was no "quiet quitting" for me, but there *was* a planned strategy.

The stock price—as it always does—aggressively reacted to any move by the company.

One day, you thought you were rich.

The next day, you could have lost it all.

I slowly started a drip campaign of selling my shares to not raise my own red flag for the company to see. I needed to hold on as long as possible.

Eric would be gone at the beginning of the second quarter. This was faster than expected, which heightened the urgency to define my exit.

Even though the stock options were ours, the CEO tracked the sale of all options and saw it as *disloyal,* which could potentially throw a wrench in my grand plan.

In January, I found out that a number of my peers were dumping their stock, so I needed to act fast to not lose out.

The goal is to always buy low and sell high.

Or earn stock options low and sell high.

The company had just reached a high-water mark in January. I had no experience with stock before, so I had no idea what I should do with it. I just assumed I would ride it out until the company was sold and then really make some money.

But my friends advised me differently, thank God.

They recommended that I take chunks at a time to pay for things that were most important: mortgage, car loans, and college tuition savings for the kids. Get big items out of the way to then start building wealth.

Well, shit.

I had not done that at all, and we were sitting at a high stock price. I was getting nervous. On paper I had money, but not in the bank, and it wasn't quite enough to feel comfortable floating in an abyss of uncertainty. I had sold some shares to help pay for the house, but that was not enough.

I needed to unload it all and pray that it would leave enough of a margin to scrape by until the full dream of building a business could be actualized.

Our financial advisor did not recommend a "panic sell" because it would cause, well, panic.

And when investors panic, stock prices drop, and everyone goes down with the ship.

Now, I didn't have enough options to start a *true* panic, but I didn't want to bring myself out from under the radar either.

The company was too volatile and could not handle a stock panic. Publicly, we were waiting for a new product launch and the accompanying data and analysis. Privately . . . it was a firestorm of a revolving door of employees and management who did not handle anything well.

If the CEO sneezed wrong, the stock could take a hit.

Back to drip-selling it was.

The stock value bounced all over the place as I was slowly selling off shares. We all held our breath, waiting for the new product to skyrocket share prices. If that happened, I would be stuffing the mattress with cash.

If that happened.

⌇

I have always been an early riser. That fateful day was no different.

Get up.

Workout.

Get the day rolling.

It was a warm spring day in April.

Eric was gone, and I was dancing in my own exit anticipation.

I checked the market news and saw that our company was going to have a press conference to discuss the data release for the new product. The call was going to take place at 11:00 a.m.

It was going to be a great day. I just knew it.

Apparently, though, I knew nothing.

The drug did not do what it was supposed to be doing at this point of the trial, and the continuation of the study would be evaluated.

Simply put, the product was a dud.

Boom.

There it was.

The company dropped a big bomb, and the stock price took a huge hit. It dropped by more than 50 percent in mere minutes.

My share-selling drip campaign was moot. Some of my options were now underwater, worth less than what I owned them at.

This was bad.

Really, *really* bad.

Now, I would have to play the waiting game a bit longer and see if I could salvage any value of my shares.

Shit.

Shit!

Shit!!!

I wanted out so bad I could taste it, but my hope for freedom was smashed in the blink of an eye. My head was spinning. But I needed to be smart, calculated, and purposeful. The exit strategy had to pause. People started to jump ship. Management was in chaos.

As much as I wanted out, as much as I *needed* out, I couldn't just think of myself.

I had to think about Lisa.

I had to think about our boys.

Our future.

I had to make it work.

Spring turned into summer. And the rise in temperature was finally matched by the rise in stock prices.

I kept my head down and my work streamlined. It was finally time to all-out sell.

That was it.

My final stand at that company.

For months behind the scenes, I was not simply strategizing stock selling. I was strategizing for the big *next*.

While still at the company, I had an assistant director of training, Jack.

Good friend.

Great guy.

Excellent leader.

He and I got into cahoots over what we should do with our lives. He also had a flair for the entrepreneurial spirit, and we started making plans. Nothing too crazy, just a lot of shoptalk.

I think we both wanted to boost each other's confidence and see if we could actually make something work.

Jack was even in for the diaper bag idea, even though that never went anywhere, and he had no kids, and we most likely weren't going to have more either.

But it was a blast.

The reality of jumping ship and starting a *training* business from scratch wasn't all just fun and games. Sure, we both had the experience, but there were real financial risks involved. I worried that because I had a new house and two kids, *my* risk of putting up money while having zero income was higher than Jack's. I worried there was a discrepancy in our "all in" attitude.

The pressure felt immense.

We spent months and months trying to align things as much as possible, but as much as we could talk in circles, we knew that most of the unknown could only be answered by the actual doing of the job. If we waited until we were 100 percent ready, we would never do it.

We knew our profession. We knew our capabilities. We knew it was time.

I had to make it work.

We both decided to walk away from our jobs in July.

The stage was set.

CHAPTER 14

The Alkemist

O ne of the hardest things about starting a business is not the money
or the risk or the suffocating fear of failure.

It's choosing a name.

When I first met Jack, it was—of course—through a work event. I had
heard about him through a friend of mine and Lisa's, who was our third
musketeer and also worked in the industry. She told us all about this new
guy she was seeing—one of our training partners from another company.
They were getting serious.

I appointed myself the role of de facto big brother and told her that he
better treat her right.

Or else.

I eventually met Jack at some function or another. There was a group of
us in training, and there he was, chest puffed and eyes inscrutable.

"You want to step outside?"

Our friendship was immediate.

When we had to choose a name for our blossoming training company, the name came quickly to us.

Step Outside.

It had two levels of interpretation. The first—stepping outside, ready for a fight (in the best ways possible, of course). The second—stepping outside of the box. We liked both and it felt natural. We were ready for this fight, and we wanted to convince people to step outside of their typical training routines and think outside the box with us.

We ran the name by several of our friends, confident in a resounding *hip, hip, hooray.*

That didn't happen.

"Yeah, no, that's not going to work."

The actual consensus by our friends—both people in the industry and training world—was that sure, the name had meaning for *us*, but it didn't mean anything to anyone else.

We went back to the drawing board. There were a lot of dud ideas thrown into the mix, but we knew that if we kept digging, we would strike perfect-name gold.

To make something out of nothing is magic. And that's what we were doing. Or, at least, that's what we were *trying* to do.

It was alchemical.

It became *Alkemy Partners.*

K for Kaveney.

P for Jack's last name.

And Lisa. Lisa was going to run operations from the start, supporting the success of the blossoming business.

We filed and formed the LLC for Alkemy Partners on June 28 in New Hampshire. The state motto of "Live Free or Die" resonated strongly. We finally had a name, legal structure, branding, and business cards.

We were focused on training *and* marketing. We were embarking on something entirely new in the life sciences world.

Now, most new companies would probably have a book of business lined up and ready to go by launch day.

But not us.

We had prospects but nothing confirmed.

Foolish?

Maybe.

But we hesitated to go knocking on doors while still employed during the preparation stages of the business. There was an unethical air with double-dipping, and neither of us felt comfortable starting off the new venture by burning bridges with the old. This was not a risk we were going to take. So, not having *any* new business was the lesser of two evils.

We still kept in contact with Eric after he was no longer with the company, and he made some connections for us with a guy who worked at a midsize pharma company. Eric arranged a meeting for us, and our first sales pitch was on the books.

The Fourth of July holiday was just a few days away. The catalyst for the launch of our successful business was upon us.

Jack and I met in New Jersey on July 1 at the hotel next to our prospective first client. We had both resigned that day. Jack handed in his notice to me (as I was still his superior at the time), and I handed in both of our notices to HR.

That was it.

Our careers were over.

Our new venture lay ahead.

I had to make it work.

The meeting was set for 10:00 a.m. on July 3. The company was shutting down at noon for the holiday. We had stayed up late the previous two nights strategizing, going over our slides, and refining our tactic. We had playfully gained new nicknames from a mutual friend upon this endeavor: Show Pony and Workhorse.

I was the show pony.

Jack was the workhorse.

We had our roles.

We both had our hearts in it.

We just needed a chance.

We walked into the building in standard pharmaceutical attire: suit and tie, shined shoes, and a briefcase full of everything you would need to run the business out of your car because, at this point, we were.

I introduced us to the security team inside the lobby.

"I am Jim, and this is Jack with Alkemy Partners. We are here to see Craig."

That was it, our first official announcement of who we were. It sounded *awesome.*

We walked to the conference room, got set up, and waited for the decision-makers to show up.

First up, the marketing team. We met and discussed our history and what we were hoping to do. Nice conversation.

But it was the training team that would make the decision on who they would work with. The director and two of her training managers walked in. Pleasantries were exchanged, and we dove in.

"What do you specialize in?" the director asked.

"Training, oncology training."

"Do you build workshops or modules or both?"

"We do both."

"How?"

Well . . .

Given that we were literally only hours old, we hadn't yet built any modules for Alkemy. We had built hundreds of modules for the industry, just not yet under our new company name. We had every capability of actualizing everything we promised as a company; we just hadn't yet had the ability to execute. After a bit, the two training managers peeled out of the meeting. It was time for vacation. The director stayed behind and peppered us with a few more questions.

"How long have you been in business? Do you have any examples of your work?"

The intensity of her tone and questions was getting serious; not condescending, but maybe a bit passive-aggressive . . . as if we were wasting her time.

Then she threw a verbal dagger across the table.

"How many accounts do you have?"

Here goes nothing.

"Zero, we are hoping you would be our first."

"So you have no accounts, no examples of capabilities, and you just started your business yesterday?"

"Yep, that is correct."

"Well, maybe you should have had something lined up before you quit your training jobs."

I quickly responded that we did not want to double-dip while still employed elsewhere.

She applauded our *ethical* approach but not our brazenness. She would have done things differently.

No shit, Sherlock.

She promised to leave the door open in case something opened down the road. She was headed on vacation, but we should feel free to reach out in a few weeks.

Well.

It was a start.

She would leave the door open.

That would be enough to keep me going, at least for that moment.

Jack and I parted ways for our own Fourth of July holiday. I had a four-hour drive back to New Hampshire—a drive that would become my business development loop from that day forward. He jumped on a plane and headed back to Florida.

I spent those four hours reliving the meeting over and over.

All the words exchanged—good, bad, or indifferent—circled in my brain over and over like a crazy feedback loop from hell. Nothing good ever came out of that kind of thinking.

I had to make it work.

That was a long four hours.

But it was only day one. I was free, in complete control of my own destiny. My heart was all in. Business was not going to come to us—we needed to go out and get it.

As my drive took me back north, I focused on the beautiful summer evening. The beautiful family waiting for me at home. The beauty of serendipity that our Alkemy LLC was formed on June 28, exactly one year to the date of closing on our house in New Hampshire.

I told myself that the stars were aligned for a reason.

It was going to be OK.

I had to make it work.

My mind finally quieted as my heart picked up speed. I was excited.

Part
three

CHAPTER 15

The Rhythm Was No Dancer

A s the saying goes: The easiest way to make God laugh? Tell Him your plans.

Life moved forward. Lisa and I hit a groove in the new house with the kids and our routines. I was committed to the health of our work-life balance and my own physical health. The years' worth of stress over job, no job, new job, no job, and back again was starting to take its toll.

I started working out more.

Which meant a higher intake of fluids.

Resulting in more middle-of-the-night trips to the bathroom.

Lovely.

I started to notice that on more than one occasion, my middle-of-the-night zombie walk to the bathroom was not a smooth one. I felt dizzy getting out of bed and had to hold myself upright by clinging to the dresser, the bedframe, or anything that wasn't moving.

I assumed it was my blood pressure from getting out of bed too quickly. After about thirty seconds each time, the dizziness went away.

The lightheadedness came without any sort of warning or pattern. Some nights were fine.

Other nights, my head was swimming.

Ghosts of "It's probably just a monitor issue . . ." threatened to haunt my nights.

I knew I had been stressed. Doctors and scientists are still discovering all the ways in which stress can impact and manifest itself in your *physical* body. It's not always just a matter of tossing and turning and fidgeting when you've got a lot on your mind. Sometimes, it's long-term, *actual*, physical effects.

I switched out my routine and opted to drink less water. It was a simple solution.

Less water = less middle-of-the-night bathroom runs = less middle-of-the-night dizzy spells.

My math was genius.

The easiest way to make God laugh? Tell Him your plans.

Invariably, I did not factor human error into my equation. Even on nights I went to bed parched, I still sometimes had to get up. And I always had to get out of bed eventually anyway. And when I did, lightheadedness came with it.

On one particularly chilly February morning, I set my alarm for 5:30 to sneak in a workout before my sons woke.

I sat up.

Swung my legs to the side of the bed.

Feet on the ground.

One big six-foot-six-length step after another.

My head swam.

My vision blurred.

I was going down, nobody yelled timber, and I fully collapsed.

Lisa jerked awake from her sleep and looked around the room. She couldn't see me flat on the ground.

"Jim? What are you doing? Did you pass out? Just get back in bed."

It may sound flippant, but I knew my wife. There was concern in her words. I literally crawled back into bed and into her warm embrace. I scared both of us. And I didn't like it.

I had never passed out before. Not like that. I told myself that I had it all under control. I was in great shape; it was a one-time thing. I had everything under control.

The easiest way to make God laugh? Tell Him your plans.

When you are parents, your house becomes a petri dish for every communicable illness you could think of.

Both of my kids came down with hand-foot-mouth disease, which thankfully came and went pretty quickly.

But not before taking me down with it.

I came down with a severe sore throat, one of the worst I had ever had. The pain was like swallowing a box of razor blades. I did my usual home remedies, but to no avail. I self-diagnosed a strep infection, but I needed to confirm it with a doctor. I needed an antibiotic.

Because we were still new to the area, I had to find myself a new doctor. I quickly found myself one who did a quick rapid culture for strep, and while we waited, we got to know each other.

I let it slip that I had been dizzy, experienced some heart palpitations, and even passed out.

Well, the mood in the room rapidly changed.

He swung open the exam room door and called out to a nurse to bring in an EKG machine. The next thing I knew, my routine strep test turned into twelve wires attached to my body and a long sheet of paper printing from the machine.

Confirming that I had a normal sinus rhythm.

I was both a little peeved and relieved. This response from him felt like overkill when I really just needed an antibiotic for my throat. And the machine proved in that moment that I was, in fact, fine. The lightheadedness was a fluke. An "issue with the monitor," so to speak.

My heart was beating as it should.

My doctor was not as convinced. He wanted to put me through a Holter monitor assessment to rule out anything missed by the EKG.

Just a precaution, I was sure.

Not everyone was as good as me at talking themselves into a particular version of reality. I had perfected telling myself that *everything would be fine* over the years. I was sure this precaution was truly no more than that.

My strep test came back negative.

But hand-foot-mouth was confirmed.

The easiest way to make God laugh? Tell Him your plans.

I had to wear the Holter monitor for forty-eight hours while it did as the name implied . . . monitored my heart.

My kids thought I sounded like a robot. The beeping monitor noises sounded like a fax machine coming out of my chest. I had an initial office supplies jump-scare at the sound but quickly adjusted.

Throughout the process of monitoring, I was acutely aware of my heartbeat more than ever before in my life.

Did it always jump around this much?

Was it acting up more than usual because I was nervous?

Was I just imagining phantom irregularities?

One of the biggest misconceptions about the life sciences industry is that we all know what every condition of the body looks like and means. But I specialized in oncology training programs, which had absolutely *nothing* to do with men's heart health. How was I supposed to know what any of this beeping indicated?

My test period was over. I called into the Holter monitor clinic because back in the day there wasn't an app to track these kinds of things on. Remote monitoring was just coming into the market and was not mainstream just yet.

I literally had to hold the phone up to the device so the nurse on the other line could listen in. If I wasn't so nervous, I would have laughed at the image.

Listening party over, the nurse paused on the line.

"Sir, where are you?"

"On the couch . . ."

"OK, stay there. The doctor will call you right away."

Well, shit.

I was no expert, but I knew it couldn't be good. Lisa joined me on the couch and held my hand as we awaited the doctor's call.

"Mr. Kaveney? I am officially diagnosing you with paroxysmal atrial fibrillation."

My doctor interpreted what my body had been trying to communicate.

My heart was not happy.

My head swam. This time, not from dizzying lightheadedness, but from all the questions about what was happening to me.

My heart raced. This time, not from a medical condition, but from the panic over what my future would look like with a heart condition.

The irregular, rapid heartbeat led to me passing out, feeling weak, and out of breath. Thankfully, it did not happen all the time. But the Holter monitor showed that it was beginning to happen more frequently. This was just the beginning.

And so, my journey with atrial fibrillation began. Right as I was venturing out on this new career path. Atrial fibrillation wasn't a death sentence; it was manageable.

Symptoms could come and go.

It was treatable.

It wasn't the end of life as I knew it.

It wasn't the worst health news someone could be dealt.

It was . . . a lot to process.

A heart condition.

Funny.

I was all "heart" when it came to work. My heart ran my decision-making process. My heart was my signpost for whether I was on the right path. My heart was the thing that guided me through feelings of uncertainty. My heart was . . .

Unwell.

I told myself I would be A-OK with my new AFib.

I had to make it work.

But . . . I also couldn't be passing out when soliciting new business. Or when walking up the stairs. Or, God forbid, when driving. I had to get this thing under control.

The easiest way to make God laugh? Tell Him your plans.

In an attempt to control my heart rate, the doctor put me on a beta-blocker. Prior to this, I never took any long-term medicine except for my rounds of medicine as a sick child and my daily adult aspirin. But, throwing the beta-blocker into the mix wreaked havoc on my carefully scheduled life. They were sure they could fix my problems medically. I was a low-risk candidate for a stroke, so I didn't need a procedure.

I wanted the drug to make a difference.

I wanted it to be a miracle. Making something out of nothing. Maybe, just maybe, this medication would make everything better.

But . . . it made my life worse.

This was the standard medical path, and for many people, it works great. But me? I felt like shit. I was walking up the stairs like an old man, struggling to catch my breath, and my heart rate was *way* too low.

I rode out the medicine a bit longer to see if the adjustment period corrected itself. It did not. I called my doctor within a month and opted to stop the drug altogether. Feeling terrible *all* the time did not make up for feeling lightheaded *some* of the time. For me, it was not worth it, mentally, physically, or emotionally. By ditching the medicine, I once again felt like myself.

The last time there was a probable "monitor issue," I had to really talk myself into not panicking.

Just one more stroke.

Well, if the Holter monitor was not a fluke and I was not at risk for an actual medical stroke, maybe I could find solace in my old workout habits. Maybe I could find solace in the water.

I hadn't completely given up rowing after college. When we lived in Connecticut, I loved taking a boat out on the Connecticut River. The muscle memory never left, and there was still nothing better than the slip of water around the oars' movement.

The fateful Fourth of July weekend and the launch of Alkemy Partners came and went.

Sure, I had a brewing cardiac issue, but it was nothing a little beach time with the kids couldn't cure. Didn't I say I was the best at talking myself out of a panic situation? I was sure a day off could heal any ailment. Where there was beach, there was water. And where there was water . . . there was likely to be rowers.

The beach was a little less than to be desired, but it did the trick. It was a small-town beach, and there was water.

Flat water.

As I looked out, all I could see were rowing shells gliding across the smooth surface.

The only problem? There weren't actually any rowers or boats on the water . . .

My mind was placing them there. And my mind was racing.

This town needed a rowing team, and I was going to start it.

I did not really know anyone yet in the town, but I was going to start making calls. I learned that there was an attempt to start a rowing program before, but it failed. Undeterred, I started to lay the foundation within the community by talking with the town recreation, the high school athletic director, and even the board of directors for the local lake association.

Through my reaching out to the high school, I connected with one of the student counselors—Tim—who had extensive experience in rowing. He was happy to jump in and help where he could, making connections. We both had the mind for rowing, and my heart sure needed to stay at a non-stroke risk.

I launched a for-profit training company and a nonprofit community rowing program.

Guess which one took off faster than you can say "row"?

My vision to bring a rowing program to my town eventually picked up. One of my neighbors ran a full-page article to bring rowing to the lake for a learn-to-row program over the summer.

I needed some help. Within a few days of the article posting, so many people reached out asking how they could help. I made connections with other rowing programs in the area and borrowed their equipment to execute the learn-to-row.

We needed to assess if there was any real community interest. We planned both adult and kids learn-to-row sessions at 5:30 in the morning. That was the only time we could use the town beach because of camps and other summer lake activities.

People thought we were nuts.

I was used to that.

I told myself that the people would come.

And come they did.

We had eight youth rowers and five adults. Plenty of people to get it going. We ran the program for two weeks with great success. We proved to the community that there was interest. We quickly established a board of directors and brought in coaches for the program. I was on cloud nine.

But.

I was at the grind all day working to build my business and then coaching rowing at night. On the calm, smooth surface, everything looked balanced. Work hard, play hard, work harder.

Below the surface, the water was churning, and I was struggling to get anything going that would actually provide the financial means to sustain my family.

I wanted to do both.

Just one more stroke.

I had to make it work.

The easiest way to make God laugh? Tell Him your plans.

Something needed to change.

As much as I like to consider myself capable of doing a million things at once and being the king of juggling responsibilities, reality sometimes knocks you on your ass.

My physical capabilities weren't what they used to be. I knew I wasn't twenty anymore, but I had hoped that my body could withstand all the strain of a busy life.

My heart was desperate to be a part of this community program. My heart was also screaming at me to *stop* any time I even got close to overexertion.

As much as it broke my already temperamental heart, I had to pull back from rowing. But I had at least *established* the thing. Brought my personal saving grace to the community. Been a part of its founding and pushed it out of the proverbial nest to fly on its own.

But it wasn't on its own.

It was uplifted by the talents of the community who took the reins and ran with it.

And although I could no longer be "on the ground" with everyone, I remained on the board of directors and oversaw its progress as the program blossomed. And boy, did it blossom. We had established the high school program, managed the adult/master rowing program, and were expanding resources in the community.

My boys were too young to understand what I intended with the rowing program, but they were around it through every step. My hope was to build a program that they would one day be able to participate in, and I could be their coach.

The dream.

Even though they were still too young to participate, others in the community thrived.

We had opened an opportunity for both young and old to try something new. For some in the mature crowd, it was fulfilling a lifelong dream of wanting to row. For the youth, we would hear from the parents in both written and spoken word that the sport—our little program—had pulled their kid(s) out of their shell to try something new and form friendships where it was not thought possible.

We were changing lives.

Both psychologically and physiologically.

I wished I had had this kind of exposure to mind–body well-being as a kid. I was in the throes of despair as an eleven-year-old for reasons perennially unknown.

I wanted to ensure that no one in the community felt the same.

It's been ten years now of the rowing program with no signs of slowing down. There is more to do, but we have a great foundation. We believe that you don't have to be an athlete to learn to row, but once you row, you are an athlete. We built something incredible out of nothing.

CHAPTER 16

All by Myself

L ife was busy but incredible. My new office was set up just around the corner from the kitchen and off of the living room.

Just as I had envisioned with Lisa when trying to convince her to let me jump into the entrepreneurial waters.

It was the perfect spot.

I could quietly work on building Alkemy Partners while periodically being interrupted by my boys' little voices having fun, peeking their heads in for a hug or two. It was those hugs and the support from my wife—and her hugs too—that kept me fueled up to fight through the adversity of what it means to own and run your own business.

Jack and I came out of the gate swinging. Alkemy Partners was *the* dream.

We were making something out of nothing.

I was in New Hampshire, and he was in Florida. Jack traveled as much as possible and, being forty-five minutes outside of Boston and four hours from New York and New Jersey, we were in the pharmaceutical and biotech corner of the world.

Somebody was going to take a chance.

Somebody *had* to give us a chance.

But it's no secret in the job market that no one wants to hire you until you have experience. And you can't get experience until someone hires you.

I remembered this all too well from my days trying to break into sales.

It was a crazy hamster-wheel feedback loop. One that newly graduated college students know well.

But we weren't in college anymore. I was in my midthirties and trying to support a family. We needed something to snap us out of the rejection cycle. It was starting to feel wildly overwhelming.

Our big break finally came a few months later from a small-town barbershop, of all places.

I was at the barbershop, getting a trim and reading one of the local bimonthly newspapers. Right on the front cover was an extensive article on a pharmaceutical company based in Manchester, New Hampshire.

Incredible.

Manchester was better known for engineers and finance, not pharmaceuticals. Overwhelmed with excitement, I called the company on the spot. After a few minutes of engagement, I set up a meeting with this company.

Jack came up from Florida the following week, and we met the head of operations and the CEO.

The office did not look like anything I had seen before in pharma. It was completely unassuming, no security, no administration.

There were just three people and a couple of investors. It was weird. It was genuine. They were fighting for a vision and fighting to prove their product was worthwhile. I loved everything about it.

We spent hours with them, learning about their products, challenges, and the direction they wanted to go. It was fascinating. They truly seemed to be at the forefront of cutting-edge therapeutics by using all-natural products.

They liked our background in pharmaceuticals and were ready to get working together.

We were flying high. Who would have thought that we would land such an incredible opportunity right in my backyard?

Afterward, at the house, we were in full celebration mode. Drinks were passed. Cigars were lit. Our first line of business. *Finally.*

It had felt like a century before a door opened, and this was going to be it for us. We just knew it. This thinking was . . .

. . . quite naïve of us.

We had great conversations and verbal commitments but no written contract. Many more conversations would take place, but not one dollar would be given to us. The cherry on our celebratory cigar was snuffed out.

We were drifting into the autumn months with no business and no prospects. As we were coming out of the Great Recession, pharmaceuticals were going through a lot of layoffs and shifts in trends.

All over LinkedIn, people in the pharma world were labeling themselves as "consultants." I understood the temptation. You could list yourself as a "consultant" in whatever capacity you wanted, convince someone you're an expert, and make some cash while biding time until the next full-time position became available.

I didn't necessarily blame anyone for this, but what was, for many, nothing more than a trend was a full-time job for us.

That no one would hire us for.

Because we didn't have enough experience.

Because no one would hire us.

It was exhausting.

I thought I was past the saga of life that was the constant rat race of hope and rejection.

Unfortunately, we were still spinning circles in the rat race.

We had to find ways to differentiate ourselves from the consultant competitors. We pushed transparency, innovation, and long-term goals. We fought to maintain integrity amongst the frauds of promise.

We ran into several individuals and companies who were *really* excited about what we had to offer and kept promising that "when things smooth out, you guys will be the first ones we call."

But the calls never came.

I closed out the year stable.

Stable business meaning *no* business, no growth, nothing.

Stable mind. We were only six months in with nothing to worry about (yet), so giving us six months to get it up and running was an investment I was OK with. And so was Jack.

Stable heart. I was living with my atrial fibrillation, maintaining my workouts and routines.

Stable family. The most important part. Our kids were thriving and loving being around their cousins and grandparents. We weren't making any money, but our lives were richer. I was seeing the rewards of the "calling"— the divine inspiration that pulled me to want to move the family to New Hampshire—and I think the family was feeling it too.

We landed our very first project in the new year.

It was about damn time.

We had launched Alkemy Partners to be a disruptor in the pharmaceutical industry. We were building an oncology-specific training company with a heavy emphasis on integrating marketing into every aspect of what we built. We were tired of the silos in the industry where marketing and training never truly aligned to build a better sales team. Yes, there was collaboration, but never at a deep level where brands could see that every initiative could be an adjoining training program. The marketing and training stories should be intertwined. Inseparable. A domino effect of innovation.

Alkemy was going to fix this.

This project . . . didn't come our way from a long-standing connection in pharmaceuticals.

Nope.

It came from Joseph—a true master of trades who I had hired to help with some wiring in our house. He introduced me to the company he worked with doing hospital tech.

How did this small project fit into our mission statement?

In short, it didn't.

It was a small project that was a bit outside of our wheelhouse, but we were determined to make lemonade out of lemons because . . .

There was a carrot.

A big, shiny, opportunistic carrot.

We were told that if we agreed to this smaller, out-of-wheelhouse project, the door would be open for a much bigger involvement in their training operations in their health care division. That was where we wanted to go. It was a resounding "Yes."

What was a small project detour in the grand picture of lucrative training projects? We were businessmen, damn it. We weren't going to look a gift horse in the mouth.

We pulled our resources together and completed the small project.

When it was all said and done, we put $13,500 in the bank.

Great profit for a first job, but well below the standard poverty line for two people to split.

They got their small project completed; we got . . . no other phone calls from them.

The dangled carrot was gone, simply because of a hierarchical decree that Joseph could not control.

Sigh.

How many different metaphors can you come up with for a corporate bait and switch? Now take that number and multiply it. That's how disappointed we were. It was another dead end.

But . . .

It was at least *something*. We had made zero dollars up to that point, so at least there was one check made out to Alkemy Partners, and we prayed it wouldn't be the last.

We knocked on every proverbial door that we could find. Getting our name out there was important.

Networking.

Connecting the dots.

People meeting people.

People helping people.

When I panicked over the sales job in Oil City, I was told to just talk to people. Don't try and sell them anything. Make a connection and see where it goes. There I was, years later, doing the same thing to keep us afloat.

This time, I was not locked into a staring contest with a doctor's office. Instead, I was looking dead-on at startup business adversity.

There was too much on the line.

My heart and my mind knew that this was one staring contest we were *not* going to lose.

We were rolling into the second quarter, and the seasons were changing. I was hoping for a break. An opportunity was going to present itself. I could smell it in the spring air.

The easiest way to make God laugh? Tell Him your plans.

Nine months into our brand-new business, I got the call.

Jack was done.

He had to find a more stable job. He couldn't do the rat race anymore.

Um, what?

I was beyond disappointed and a bit perplexed. I had two kids and absolutely no income, and he had *none* of those pressures. But my perspective on the issue didn't matter; his mind was made up.

Within just a few days, I was working with my attorney to draw up separation of business partnership papers with Jack. I cut him a check for his half of the website money. I was numb.

The comfort of taking a huge risk with someone was over.

I was ALONE!

I had to make this work.

Not that I wasn't already, but I would officially take on the role of show pony *and* workhorse. There was no one else.

Well, there was Lisa. And that wasn't nothing. That was huge. She was helping me redefine the company, the vision. She was there every step of the way, but I couldn't help but feel the weight of responsibility to make this wild dream a wild success.

On his way out the door, my now ex-business partner uttered his famous saying: "I am always late to the party, and I always leave early."

I took this as a vote of confidence that something was going to come out of this entrepreneurial experiment.

The world was my oyster. Again . . . again.

In some ways, it was easier because I could just steer the ship at will. No need to worry about taking the temperature of someone else's decision. If Jack wasn't ready to commit all in for the long term, so be it. But I was ready. I had been ready. I'd made some good contacts over the months and knew that a solo venture would require some pivoting of the business model. That was all OK.

It was going to be OK.

I had to make this work.

There was never a better time to work on my mantras.

The next three months were nose to the pavement. I had to refine the company's mission, vision, and basic "Why?"

Why did Alkemy exist?

What was its purpose?

What was *my* purpose?

I wasn't afraid of failure for failure's sake. All I could do was give it 100 percent effort. That's all I could control, and I knew that. What I was afraid of was the pity.

The "Aw, poor guy, he tried."

The "I would have done it differently if it were me" judgment.

I wanted none of that.

Alkemy was initially founded to address the lack of communication between training and marketing. I hired a local marketing agency to help me refine my messaging, develop my new website, and make clear to the public what *exactly* they would get by hiring Alkemy.

But apparently, what they would get was still "too much."

A prospective client broke it to me gently that while my vision of integrated marketing and training were inspired, Big Pharma wasn't ready for it yet.

I had to choose one over the other.

I needed a singular widget that was going to make people pounce.

Oh, and I still had no case studies of successful outcomes because of the whole loophole-from-hell problem.

The choice moving forward was clear.

I chose training. It *had* to be training. I still believed wholeheartedly in my vision for Alkemy, but if I had to rebrand, it would be under the umbrella of my own innovation. I stripped Alkemy down to next to nothing and then, like magic, rebuilt it into something that was more easily digestible for clients.

Historical Perspective of the Management of the Disease State.

HPMDS.

The first thing I created out of nothing.

I believed in a new approach to training and had done something tangible with it at the old company.

I don't think it was *foolish* for my partner and me to leap into the vast unknown when we did, flying by the seat of our pants.

But I do think that the feedback was spot on: The company mission had to be tight. There were so many ideas, goals, and visions we had for this thing that we had a hard time letting our words catch up with our brains.

For Alkemy Partners 2.0, I took several steps back.

I was a man of science. I was an educator. I was a salesman. I was a businessman. I was a leader. I was an innovator.

Bringing disparate ideas together is what I am best at, and I knew I had to bring all of these parts of myself together in a streamlined manner.

The rebranding of the company was almost complete.

I just needed to do the same for myself.

For the past decade in pharma, my professional look was all suits and ties, but Lisa would make a recommendation partially based on my fashion laziness and the need to make a statement.

After letting my facial hair grow out during the rebuilding process, Lisa recommended keeping the beard and adding in a bowtie. The suits would go away, replaced with a younger-looking blazer, beard, and bowtie. This would become my signature style. So much so that if and when I deviated from it, my clients would call me out. The brand was complete.

The *Kaveney Work Ethic* now went nicely with the Kaveney Work *Look.*

CHAPTER 17

Bubbles and Bud

The Goose to my Maverick was gone.

Not *gone* gone.

It wasn't that dramatic.

It was just a dissolution of a business partnership.

It was a wild risk that was no longer mutually beneficial.

It was . . . leaving me all ALONE! in a two-person jet plane flying wildly out of control with no landing strip in sight.

I struggled with how to safely bring a spiraling ball of fire back to the ground. Back to reality.

The only thing I could think of to try and ground my panic?

A six-pack of Budweiser Long Necks.

And a good book.

And . . . a bubble bath.

Hear me out. I wasn't normally one for a bubble bath, but Lisa always insisted it was the "perfect" place to kick back and relax, so I eventually acquiesced.

On one such occasion, my bubble bath reading changed the entire course of my life.

It was a warm summer night. I was three hours into my four-hour drive home from New Jersey.

I was exhausted, my head was spinning, and my go-to mantras weren't quite doing it anymore. I was once again driving home without bringing any proverbial bacon.

I got a phone call from my friend Doug, who quite possibly could be one of the smartest guys I know. A brilliant medical and business mind. As happens in life, we hadn't talked in a while and took the time to catch up.

It was nice not being ALONE! with my thoughts for the last part of my drive.

After the usual pleasantries, Doug's tone took on that of a sincere business advisor.

I explained to him how my business partner left, and I was on my own, reconfiguring the company and trying to gain traction anywhere I could get it.

"So, you have not read the book yet?" he asked.

What book?

"*Think and Grow Rich* by Napoleon Hill—it is seen as being America's first self-help book for entrepreneurs."

I hadn't read it. But if Doug recommended it, I would read it. It was available on any of the book apps for just a few bucks, and Doug promised it would be the best five bucks I'd ever spent.

The house was quiet and empty when I got back. Lisa and the boys were out with the extended family, getting ice cream and enjoying their summer.

This was usually the perfect recipe for my intrusive thoughts, but I was determined not to let the shadows of ALONE! haunt me that night.

I grabbed a six-pack of beer, purchased *Think and Grow Rich* online, and turned on the water. It was always a feat of aerobics to get my six-foot-six self into the tub. But I didn't care. There was no judgment tonight.

Any leftover tension and stress from the day melted away once I hit the hot water. With my body relaxing and a cold beer in my hand, I began to read the book.

No.

Devour the book.

The book.

Within the first few pages I was immediately hooked. I consumed the pages at a pace that I had never done before. I liked to read, but not like this.

With each turn of the page, I found myself getting more excited that I was on the right track. I was checking the boxes for what needed to be done to launch a business.

I was doing it.

The book.

It put words to my hopes and fears. Helped me qualify what it was that I was doing. I mildly regretted the fact that I hadn't read this book before starting a business, but there was no time to look back.

While the title is *Think and Grow Rich*, in my mind it wasn't all about money. It was about feeding the desire to accomplish something. To see my efforts transform into something worthwhile to me, my family, and the world.

Again, I had all the capability in the world; I just needed the opportunity to prove my ability.

Most days, I felt like a chicken running around with its head cut off while simultaneously trying to change the world. This book gave me a blueprint.

Two hundred thirty-eight pages.

Four beers.

Several drops in temperature.

The house was still quiet, and my skin was pruned, but I was renewed.

My bubble bath felt like a true entrepreneurial baptism.

THE f*cking book.

The next day I called my friend and former boss, Eric. I had to tell him about this book. I had to tell the world about this book. (The world sorta already knew about it, but I was pumped.)

Eric could sense the excitement and energy in my voice when talking about the details of *the book*. I told him about all the reasons he needed to read it and shared with him the story in the book that gave me literal chills. And not the kind of chills from tepid bath water.

The very first story was about a man who had an incredible passion not only to work with Thomas Edison but also to be his business partner. But the man lived in Florida and would have to somehow get to New Jersey. He was poor and had no formal training and would start by sweeping Edison's floors. In time, he would become Edison's greatest asset.

The man's name was Edwin, and he moved to Orange, New Jersey, for his new job.

My version of Edwin, Eric, had also just moved to New Jersey for his new pharma job.

"What, what, what, what?!" he screeched over the phone.

The coincidence was crazy. And we both saw it as much more than a coincidence.

It was go-time.

Even though I had made very little money at this point, I had to set a goal to achieve. That morning, I wrote down on a piece of paper and displayed on my desk the amount of money Alkemy was going to bring in revenue by my fifth year of business.

$1.5 million.

Why?

Because it wasn't a crazy value in the life sciences world. And I figured that if I crossed the million-dollar marker, another company would come along to buy me out.

Sure, I'd only made $13K by that point and lost half of it when my business partner left.

But I just needed to "think" the right thoughts and then become "rich."

I would like to say that the business transformation happened overnight. It didn't.

But I was focused on being "success conscious" and not "failure conscious."

As Henry Ford said, "Whether you think you can or you think you can't—you're right." So that was it. I had to think more about the successes that were coming and less about the successes not.

I was starting to finally get some breaks. More doors opened.

The *Kaveney Work Ethic* was in full swing.

Unfortunately, the revolving door of global pharmaceuticals really didn't give two shits about my personal work ethic.

Doors were closed for reasons beyond my control.

A product was pulled from the market.

The FDA didn't grant approval.

Another company launched a too similar product first.

More trials with better results were needed.

I could throw every hour of my day into working on project proposals for potential clients, but if the market said "jump," there was nothing I could do.

Financial concerns started to bubble up in our family life.

Money and health insurance.

The two greatest nemeses of entrepreneurs.

Lisa had to step in and help. She, who had left her amazing job after my encouragement, now had to take on night work to support my dreams.

A saint, my wife.

Months passed since my life-changing bubble bath, and soon it was December. Eric had given me a bit more business working with his new company, and I was doing some training consulting gigs for what would become one of my competitors.

I had to swallow my pride.

I was now a year and a half into getting the business "going."

There were signs of potential success, but you really had to squint way off in the distance to see them.

A few weeks before Christmas, Lisa came into my office with her sweet and supportive voice.

"I think you have about six more months of this experiment. We need some true, stable income."

Still a saint.

I couldn't argue with her. I was disappointed. But she was right. Naturally.

I know you can "only fail if you don't try," but I was both trying *and* failing.

We had our first come-to-Jesus meeting. She had been patient for eighteen months with a lot of nonstarters. A few odd jobs here and there didn't come nearly as close to what we needed as a family as I would have liked.

People who I thought would be in my corner and throw me some help disappeared. Industry friends dissolved back into the woodwork when it didn't seem like Alkemy was going anywhere. I reached out to everyone I had worked with in the past who I figured would be in my corner. I wanted to connect *some* dots, at least, but to no avail.

Did it sting?

Like a bee.

The *Kaveney Work Ethic* didn't necessarily expect any handouts (if my mother found out, she would probably wag her finger at me all the way from Erie), but I also didn't expect total isolation in my venture.

Lisa supported me, of course, but I was the only one supporting Alkemy. ALONE!

So, six more months it was. I wouldn't let this reality sink me. There was too much to do. Too much to look forward to. I was determined to keep my sight high and my spirits higher.

CHAPTER 18

A Christmas Miracle

To make something out of nothing is a *motherf*cking* miracle. *Alkemy.*

Six months to turn water into wine.

Connections into dollars.

Visions into reality.

About a week after my come-to-Jesus meeting with Lisa, I got a call from two of my friends. These were—and still are—salt-of-the-earth guys.

They were technically my competition, but Alkemy was so small that "competition" might have been insulting . . . to them.

One of their clients was going through some serious changes and needed an expert in oncology training.

The easiest way to make God laugh? Tell Him your plans.

Their clients were not unfamiliar to me. I wanted to laugh. They were the same company that my previous business partner and I had pitched on day one of Alkemy. Our Fourth of July rejectors.

Their leadership team, the ones I met, all left the company, leaving some pretty large gaps in their operations. They needed some serious help.

"Do you think you could meet with them?"

I did not have to think twice.

It was the days before Christmas, and all through the house, James Kaveney was cheering: Alkemy was no longer a mouse.

No, I didn't actually cheer like mice. But *damn*. I was pumped.

When one domino falls, the rest fall with it.

In this case, my loophole from hell was finally ending.

I was inspired by *the book*, and 2014 was looking up.

I was introduced to Sam, who introduced me to Dina, who gave me my first six-month contract.

Game, set, and match.

My six-month ultimatum ran head-first into an opportunity. I couldn't believe it.

I was also scared *shitless*. Eighteen months was a long time to talk myself and my company up to people. I could no longer rely on just projections and models. I now actually had to deliver.

While this new business was lining up, I was also working with Eric at his new company. He needed a head of training but couldn't afford a full-time employee, so he hired me.

I felt like a true alchemist. There had been nothing; suddenly, there were plenty of somethings.

At one-and-a-half years old, Alkemy was truly born in 2014.

The new contracts kept me very busy. Everything that I had focused on and prayed for was coming to fruition. Except the little office next to the kitchen was no longer cutting it.

If I wasn't living in New Jersey at the Courtyard by Marriott, I was living virtually for my clients.

My schedule was nuts.

Sunday night: Eat dinner with the family before heading out on the four-hour journey south to New Jersey. Check in to Courtyard by Marriott.

Monday–Thursday: Work. Work. Work. Work.

Thursday night: Drive four hours north and arrive home after the boys were already in bed.

Friday: Work.

Friday night–Sunday night: Absorb every single second with Lisa and the boys.

Wash, rinse, and repeat.

The easiest words to describe this time are *grueling* and *exhilarating*. It was no walk in the park, and I struggled to be anything other than a couch potato when I was home. I needed to be fully present over the weekend for my family, but I also needed to be away from them to keep the money flowing. I tried not to dwell on their absence while away, and thankfully, the work was consuming enough to distract me from the ALONE! nights four days a week.

At home, we moved my workspace away from the kitchen and up to the unfinished space above our garage.

I was *moving on up*.

It was insulated, but there was no heat.

My desk was a six-foot plastic table. I used a space heater under the table for warmth and would wrap my waist in a blanket. Lisa bought me a wooden privacy screen to cover the Pink Panther insulation behind me. With a little visual smoke and mirrors, no one over the computer would know otherwise. I was all business up top and all pajama bottoms and slippers below.

I had officially made it.

The six-month contract felt like I had won the lottery. But it had the potential to not be renewed after it had run its course. It was terrifying, but I had to focus on the success. Not the potential for more failure.

Lisa's ultimatum was assuaged by the new opportunities, so *that* pressure was off, but I wanted to ensure the momentum. I didn't want to go backward now that I was finally getting somewhere.

I made myself indispensable to the client. I worked alongside an account lead, Carole, who became my partner in crime in salvaging what was left of their company. She had the resources to build everything, and I brought the street cred of having worked in the oncology marketplace for so many years. The collaboration was ideal. Just what I needed to get things moving.

We worked our asses off to right the ship for the client, and we built great relationships.

I was constantly reminded that my contract would *not* go beyond six months. I tried to reframe that as a challenge rather than a given.

With one month left, they extended the contract another six months.

They have now been clients of Alkemy for nine years.

The next step in building Alkemy's infrastructure was launching our mobile learning platform for advanced engagement.

Some *fancy shit* right there.

With my partners, I had a fully functioning training platform by the fall of 2014.

The foundation of the company was growing.

I did not have any customers for it yet, but it set me up for when the time was right.

And, oh, was it coming.

By fall 2014, I was in desperate need of additional resources. A client needed additional advanced clinical oncology training support. I was already putting in eighty hours a week.

I was tapped out.

It was time to hire someone.

But I couldn't exactly *afford* to hire someone. Not financially. Not yet.

Thankfully, I knew exactly who to call on.

I met Joan when I was the director of training at my last company. She had just jumped from working at one of the largest cancer centers in the world to join the industry.

She, as we often said, came to the "dark side."

She was not good at her job.

She was *great*.

But she was also modest.

A quiet winner who just liked to work and work *hard* and be the best at what she did.

When I left to start Alkemy, she said that she would follow me when the time was right. I agreed to it, of course.

She was a rock star.

In the summer of 2014, I started calling her on a regular basis, giving her the updates, and telling her I felt something was coming.

She kept telling me she was ready.

But I had no business hiring a full-time employee just yet. So, I would have to bring her on as a 1099. She knew the risks. *I* knew the risks. Neither of us went into this lightly. We just knew it was time. She was in Texas and came to Boston for meetings. I would take her to dinner to discuss what was going on, and Lisa would join. Lisa needed to meet this *Joan* who I talked so highly of.

Team Alkemy was forming.

The business would become affectionally known as the "Jim and Joan Show." While my clients always liked working with me, once they got to know Joan, they wanted her. We started telling people that Alkemy now had two offices. We'd gone national.

It was Jim and Joan and . . . Lisa, quietly guiding the business operations. Lisa hadn't yet officially joined the Alkemy team, but she was always available to help in any way she could.

See, here's the thing about my wife.

There's probably no one who works harder. And that's coming from Mr. *Kaveney Work Ethic*.

Before embracing the work of a full-time mom, Lisa worked as chief operating officer.

The *COO*.

She worked in direct patient care with behavioral and mental health at a hospital extension. She was the director of the ship. She oversaw the grant writing, instructional design, programming, employment, budgets, patient advocacy, project management, and more. She was available at all hours of the day—and night—for putting out fires and strategic maneuvering.

Countless people relied on her to keep things running smoothly.

Which, of course, she did.

She was badass.

She was the reason our family ship could run while I was off trying to once again reinvent the wheel.

She was the reason I could even keep that new wheel spinning.

She stepped in quietly at first.

She was the advisory board I didn't know I needed. The pragmatic eye on operations I absolutely needed.

Her role in Alkemy Partners was integral. I didn't see it coming that *she* would be the new partner of the namesake, but I should have known better.

Lisa.

Alkemy closed the year making quite a bit more than the previous year's $13K.

During that life-changing year, I focused my years of classes, studies, and passion for teaching and training toward a specific goal:

Building one of the best training companies in the industry.

HPMDS, baby.

I was Alkemy.

Alkemy was me.

And it was becoming a powerful force.

CHAPTER 19

Life Is a Highway

One year of success for Alkemy meant two hundred fifty days of sleeping away from home.

Eighty-hour work weeks were considered light.

We were cruising, but not without some side effects.

After two years of effectively living with my diagnosis of paroxysmal atrial fibrillation, the temporary erratic cardiac rhythms started to become more persistent.

I always felt like I was in control and didn't let the stress get the better of me. But the mind is a mysterious place. One that was most likely causing more damage to my physical health than I cared to acknowledge.

At first, I thought it was just pure exhaustion.

It did not matter where I was . . . whenever I sat down, I immediately fell asleep.

For someone who was spending countless hours on the road each week, this was a living nightmare. On too many occasions, I had to punch my legs while driving up or down I-95 just to keep myself awake. My best friend, the highway, wavered in front of me more than once as I literally had to fight myself from passing out.

Instead of *Finding Nemo's* "just keep swimming," I told myself to "just keep driving" while inflicting some pretty gnarly bruises on my thighs.

It was the best solution to my problem.

One that I chose to keep to myself.

Unfortunately, I couldn't keep it a secret for long.

Pretty much anything physical took me out.

I couldn't start my days with workouts.

I couldn't run around with my kids.

I couldn't get up the stairs without feeling like an eighty-five-year-old with emphysema.

This I could not hide from my kids or Lisa.

The belief that I could manage my AFib without any serious medical intervention was fading away. My heart was completely out of whack, and my mind was too busy trying to keep the business moving along to worry about anything else.

It was time to officially confirm with my cardiologist what I already knew.

I was officially in persistent atrial fibrillation, which happens when abnormal heart rhythm occurrences last for more than a week. It *could* eventually return to normal, but intervention was possible.

For me, it wasn't *possible.*

It was *eventual.*

And my quality of life was diminished at the ripe old age of forty.

In the spring of 2016, I was scheduled for a radiofrequency ablation. My cardiologist explained it as a simple, no-big-deal procedure. Which, for someone who *does* the procedure all the time, was probably true.

But for someone who had never had the procedure before . . . it was a big deal.

The doctor would go into my heart and create tiny scars on the back of the heart around the pulmonary veins where AFib begins with its chaotic electrical signals. They would use tiny catheters and work them through the veins or arteries in my heart to reset their normal rhythm by blocking off the electrical signals.

The medicine didn't do the trick, so this was the best next step to reversing my issues. Risks were defined, and they told me it may not even work. I might need a second procedure. But with no procedure, the risk of having a stroke was five times more likely.

Comforting words for any patient.

But I had to trust the expert.

I was dealing with the perfect cocktail of denial, ego, faith, and frustration over my condition. I was given a procedure date and told, "See you then!" I chose the route of not utilizing the medical professionals around me in my career to seek a second opinion or research my options. I did not take advantage of the resources literally at my fingertips from clients to learn more about my condition.

There are three reasons for this.

The first: I didn't want anyone to know. If I could sweep it under the rug for them, I could mentally sweep it under the rug for me. Which led to the . . .

Second: Sure, it was a heart procedure. But it's not like it was full-blown open-heart surgery. I mean, it's not like people do a deep dive into research when they need to get their wisdom teeth out. I'd be in and out of the procedure, and it was fine to treat it as such.

And third (and this is truly the most important one): There wasn't much information out there that was actually organized and, therefore, not easily navigable. Google can only take you so far when trying to research your own health. Like all patients, I was given very little in the way of resource guidance. There are obviously always pamphlets about the *condition*, but not a lot regarding the *options*. This wasn't just a "me" problem; it's a health care problem. And even though I *did* have other methods of learning around me in the industry, it all pretty much said the same thing. I didn't see much about innovative techniques or experimental treatments for something like AFib. And maybe, I just didn't know where to look.

So, I did what I did best.

Had a nice talking to myself to calm down, punched myself in the leg to stay awake, and kept on working.

Up until my procedure, I pushed through the first quarter of the year as if there was nothing wrong. I wasn't trying to "play pretend," but the business needed me. My growing team needed me. My family needed me.

Thump.

A few deep breaths every time my heart skipped a beat.

Thump.

Then back to work.

I wasn't as good at pushing through as I thought.

I eventually had to disclose some of my health issues to certain clients who saw me on a regular basis. They needed to know that I didn't *intend* to seem totally checked out at points. Besides, if I collapsed at one of their facilities, we all needed to make sure I was not a liability issue.

The first quarter of business went by in a blink. I had scheduled the ablation for the beginning of the second. Family, friends, and clients were on board.

Insurance was not.

When you run your own small business, health insurance is a little questionable. It's limiting and expensive. While my cardiologist was in New Hampshire, the electrophysiologist was not. He would be doing the procedure in Massachusetts.

Crossing state lines for a procedure requiring anesthesia.

Declined.

I would have to find an electrophysiologist in New Hampshire. I was disappointed and even more stressed, but I had no choice.

American health care is . . . what it is.

My life was literally now in the hands of God and the hands of some paper pushers.

Great odds.

There are many great reasons for living in New England.

None of which are the Patriots.

I stand by what I just said.

While I had lived in New England for almost half my life, I was (and still am) a Steelers fan.

What does that have to do with anything? Not sure. But it needed to be said somewhere.

While I didn't love being surrounded by Patriots fans in New Hampshire, I did enjoy being surrounded by some of the most esteemed academic institutions and hospitals in the Northeast.

I could not cross the border to Massachusetts, but I *did* have the only academic medical center in New Hampshire, and it ranked regionally as one of the best.

I quickly got a consultation with my new electrophysiologist, Dr. Philip.

He spent close to an hour with me, getting to know me, the challenges I had, and explained the procedure that he was doing. Based on the questions I asked and my hybrid of scientific and common-man language, he pieced together that I might have had a *little* bit of experience in health care. I could talk shop enough to understand what he was saying.

His approach to the procedure was different than my Massachusetts-based doctor. Most doctors at that time were doing radiofrequency ablation (burning and cutting off the electrical signals with scars) by isolating each pulmonary vein. On average, there are four pulmonary veins, but he explained that in some rarer cases there could be a few more.

His approach was different in that he would *not* isolate each of the pulmonary veins but rather, he would, in essence, rope off the whole back side of the heart around all of the pulmonary veins, as well as the cardiac tissue in between. His theory was that this would lead to a much longer, durable remission of atrial fibrillation.

He had been doing this procedure all over the country in Ohio, in California, and now in New Hampshire. He also liked it because it would cause less scar tissue than if he tried to isolate each vein.

I was sold.

While I was going to be another statistic in the world of men's heart health, Dr. Philip made me feel like this was a very personal journey that would contribute to his larger pool of data and research.

There was no need to cross the state border; I was going to be in good hands.

My mind was at ease.

My heart clearly wasn't doing too well.

Before I left his clinic, he put a new type of heart monitor on my chest, one that would stay on twenty-four hours a day and be able to report back to him what was going on. I was thrilled the technology had advanced enough to not have to hold the phone up to my chest to transmit data.

Within a few days, he called me.

"Hello, Mr. Kaveney? Yes, this is Dr. Philip. What are you doing right now? Be specific."

I wasn't doing anything. Just sitting at my desk.

"You are not doing anything strenuous? Running, walking, nothing?"

No?

I could picture his face from across the phone.

"Your rate is way above where you should ever be. Thankfully, it only lasted for a few seconds, but it hit close to 260 bpm."

In just a few days, he captured what I had been experiencing for months. This was my existence, and it was not feeling great.

My new ablation procedure was scheduled for May 20.

I needed spring to go fast. My quality of life was suffering. I wanted to be active with my family and dogs, but just could not do it.

I couldn't do anything really. No playing. No running. No rowing. I felt physically useless.

The only thing I could do to feel remotely useful was sit at my desk and work.

Sure, my heart rate jumped all the time, even when I was just sitting, but at least it was somewhat manageable.

Joan was busy managing her projects, and I needed to tend to mine. Support was coming into the company, and we had hired some incredible new additions to the team, but everything—training, ideas, facilitation, billing, etc.—was still all locked tight in my head.

It needed to come out, but that was not going to happen for a couple more months.

In the meantime, I worked every minute up to the very moment I was admitted to the hospital for the procedure.

The hospital was an hour and a half away from our house up north. Lisa and I made the trip up the night before to sleep in a hotel, so it was not stressful in the morning.

"Why is your laptop coming with you?" Lisa asked.

There were a few things I needed to finish up prior to going under the knife.

"You're crazy."

And maybe I was. But I also felt vulnerable and not in control of my own body. Work I could control. Emails at 5:30 a.m. before pre-op. Ensuring smooth operations while out for recovery. Keeping my clients up to speed.

Health *is* the most important thing, but I also needed to make sure the money was still coming in for the health of the family. If something were to happen to me . . .

I rarely let *those* types of thoughts intrude anymore, but I also didn't want to be stupid. The harder I worked leading up to any major procedure, the more secure my family would be.

Our insurance plan sucked. But I needed to provide a different type of insurance for my own emotional security.

Sitting up in my hospital bed, rocking out the stylish hospital cap and gown, I welcomed multiple teams of health care providers. They all were going to be doing something different for me throughout the procedure, and I had to answer all the same questions multiple times over. It seemed to go on forever, and their reactions were all the same.

"Wow, you're young to be going through AFib."

"How long has this been going on?"

"This is unusual for someone so young and not obese to go through."

"Are you using cocaine?"

They had to ask *all* the questions.

They can't practice medicine if they don't ask the questions.

A quick *no* to answer their cocaine question. Apparently, my answer wasn't good enough as they looked at Lisa for confirmation of the truth.

I was not lying.

But apparently cocaine and AFib went hand in hand for cases not fitting the other usual markers. You learn something new every day.

The parade of health care providers went on forever. I started getting antsy, wanting to get this underway. My patience was further tested when the procedure ahead of me went longer than anticipated, and they had to push mine back.

When life gives you lemons, make lemonade.

Or, in my case, make money.

Jokingly, I had Lisa put my laptop on my lap in the bed and take a picture of me. I sent the picture to my biggest clients and let them know that I was working and would be billing them while at the hospital.

Making light of an otherwise terrifying situation was the only way to keep *those* thoughts at bay. If my heart was going to race, it was going to only be physical. *Not* emotional.

Finally, it was my turn.

Lisa held my hand, we said a quick prayer, and I told her I'd see her soon. Better than ever.

Surrounded by everyone in the operating room, the questions continued.

"What's your name?"

"Date of birth?"

Etc.

They had to be sure they had the right patient on their table.

Dr. Philip arrived when everything was all set. I was fully prepped, and the oxygen mask was going on. Nervous, I was still chatting a mile a minute.

"How long will it taaaaaaaa . . ."

I had never been under anesthesia before. I had no idea what I would experience. Was I going to dream? What would I dream about? Would I know the difference between dreams and reality?

"Mr. Kaveney, this is your recovery nurse. You are coming out of anesthesia."

I felt nothing but the warmth of blankets. The procedure was done. Wow, that was faster than I thought.

Dr. Philip had a different story. As I started to gain more consciousness, he explained that my surgery was a bit trickier than originally anticipated. It took longer than they thought, but he was confident that they accomplished the goal. They were eventually able to get the AFib to stop.

Trickier?

Longer?

Eventually?

I had no concept of time.

For me, the surgery was a blip.

For Lisa, it was nine hours of waiting room hell.

During the long wait, Lisa was ALONE!, keeping the business going to keep herself distracted. She set up shop in the medical library of the hospital, creating a makeshift office—Alkemy on the road—trying to maintain a sense of normalcy in a completely abnormal situation. She watched as others waiting received word of their loved ones, more coming and going as she waited for word on my procedural outcome.

After what felt like an eternity, she appeared in the doorway out of nowhere, coming to my side to give me a kiss.

Dr. Philip explained everything to her in case my foggy brain hadn't absorbed it all. She confirmed that we all had her worried.

Her, plus my eight siblings, and her extended family . . . there were a lot of people worried.

Without any reference to time, it seemed like I may have had an easier day than all of my loved ones.

Finally, my heart was calm. A normal rhythm. It had been so long that I had forgotten what a normal resting heart rate should feel like.

We were happily and healthily discharged the next day.

My boys could not have been happier to see me, and the feeling was mutual.

Thankfully, it was the weekend. No calls to make till Monday. I wasn't jumping for joy over having to have a heart procedure, but I was sure glad for some forced downtime.

Every doctor and all the research said that I would feel amazing once the heart was back in rhythm.

And they were right.

It felt like the uncontrolled electricity that was wreaking havoc on my heart was now focused and recharging my entire body, my entire soul. It was incredible. I was forty-two and, thankfully, starting to feel forty-two.

Each day post-op, I woke up, sat up, and took my pulse. Dr. Philip told me that there could be some moments when the heart felt like it was jumping around. It was normal because my heart had been under such stress for so long.

As the days progressed and I got further away from the procedure, my confidence was rising that I had this beat. After a few quiet recovery weekends at home, we were invited to our friends' house for a drink.

No drinks for me.

But it was still a beautiful evening catching up with friends. I was feeling so peaceful. So grateful.

Thump.

Weird. My heart skipped a few aggressive beats.

Thump.

Dr. Philip told me it could happen.

Thump.

Probably an issue with the monitor?

Thump.

I didn't mention anything to Lisa. I didn't want to make a scene and ruin the evening for everyone.

Thump.

My heart rate was definitely elevated. Shit.

Thump.

By morning, the elevated pace had not slowed. I shared my concerns with Lisa, and her face showed what my mind refused to believe.

A week later, I was back on the road and in New Jersey, conducting live training events for my client.

I had sporadic episodes throughout the prior week, but a call to the doctor assured us that it was probably all part of the reset process. I was cleared for roadway travel.

The training meeting was at a little seaside town in New Jersey. Not a haven for big-time medical centers, but I did not think I would need one.

Thump.

Damn it. On the first morning of training, my heart did not let up. I had to let Eric know what was happening just in case I "went down like Frazier." Eric loved quoting from Foreman and Frazier's fight. I used his lingo to convey my message.

I was not feeling great.

I made it through one training session, but it was not getting any better.

Alarmed, I took myself to the local urgent care. Again, this was a small seaside town, and I walked into your typical, doc-in-a-box shop.

I had been through a lot at this point. Not just that day but over the last few years.

So, I nonchalantly told the front desk staff that my heart was racing uncontrollably and I needed to see the doctor. I was immediately escorted into the exam room, and within a few seconds, one of the youngest doctors I had ever seen came rushing in.

She looked like she just stepped out of residency, and this was her first day on the job. There was no introduction—she just jumped right in.

"What are your symptoms?"

"How long has this been going on?"

"Are you taking medications?"

"How did you get here?"

My personal and professional history with doctors made me exceptionally calm. I gave her all the details.

She . . . freaked out. This urgent care was not equipped for my emergency. I had to go somewhere else.

Did she not realize I was in the middle of a heart crisis and there was literally nowhere else for me to go?

I had to take the reins of my own health care advocacy that day.

I told her to call the hospital in New Hampshire directly and ask for Dr. Philip. They talked, connected me to an EKG, and she sent the results immediately over to him.

Atrial flutter.

It was official.

I was no longer in the "this is a part of your healing" phase.

Dr. Philip mentioned this could happen. A-flutter is where the atria of the heart beats far more rapidly than your ventricles. A-flutter was less common than AFib. Because AFib can be so aggressive, it often masks the underlying flutter. But because my AFib was fixed, my flutter came out for its debut with a roar.

Still over the phone, Dr. Philip gave me instructions to double the dose of my diltiazem and get back to New Hampshire, where they would schedule a cardioversion.

Great.

Paddles to the chest for shockwaves. Just what everyone hopes to hear from their doctor.

I finished off the week of training in New Jersey because I didn't want to sit at home twiddling my thumbs over a procedure that wasn't scheduled for another few weeks.

It all sucked.

I had hoped that I could put the heart issues behind me. But there we were—different issue, same disruption to my life.

The month of June thankfully flew by. Business was picking up and getting more organized now that I had a team to help grow the business. Annie, our new head of finance, watched the books like a hawk, and our good friend Chopper became one of our account managers. We would continue to add to the team every six months.

This was no longer just the Jim, Joan, and Lisa show; it was now the Alkemy Partners Show and it was fun to watch.

We reached the date of my cardioversion appointment just a few days after we celebrated Alkemy Partners' fourth anniversary.

I couldn't believe it.

Four years in business.

We only needed to get to five years and we would have overcome the odds that straddle all small businesses. The five-year mark was on its way, and I was going to make sure my heart and mind were fixed on what needed to be done.

Having never been through a cardioversion before, I had no idea what to expect.

It was not as *involved* as I thought.

A quick check-in process at the local hospital and I was escorted to a semiprivate part of the quiet emergency room. Two male nurses and a doctor explained that they would reset my heart in about five minutes, and recovery would take about forty-five minutes.

I would be on my way in no time.

Just before they put me under, I saw Lisa slowly backing away. She could watch if she wanted, but she had no intention of seeing just how far off the table my body would jump.

I wanted her to stay for all the fun, but I didn't blame her for leaving.

Before I knew it, I was unconscious.

When I made my way out of anesthesia, I only had one thing on my mind.

"How did I do? How high did I jump?"

They thought I was hilarious.

Apparently, I got pretty high. They had to shift my body back fully onto the table, as I had shifted about ten degrees in the jump when shocked, and my leg landed dangling from the table. Too bad Lisa didn't see me. Apparently, white men *can* jump.

After Lisa's return and a quick waiting period, we were on our way.

Cautious optimism ruled my days.

Then weeks.

Then months.

It had been almost eight weeks since my cardioversion, and my local cardiologist wanted to get a monitor on me to see how things were going.

Prior to my departure to the doctor's office, Lisa was packing up the boys to go to our friend's house for the day. My appointment was at 11:00 a.m., so I told her that I would come home, eat some lunch, and do some yard work.

I was feeling pretty good at this point.

And it wasn't just because I was *telling* myself I was fine.

The cardioversion was holding.

Thank God.

I told Lisa I was going to clean up the raised gardens. Between work and my cardiac issues, our garden was looking more unruly by the day. The weeds needed whacking. The hedges needed trimming. The works.

Was gardening an absolute necessity of the day?

No.

But since my insides were feeling great, I wanted the outsides to match.

At the appointment with my local cardiologist, he couldn't have been giddier.

I, Jim Kaveney, was going to be the first patient in his office to try out the newest cardiac monitor on the market.

I would not have to use the antiquated Holter monitor anymore. He was going to hand me a brand-new Galaxy phone.

At the time, this phone would connect to the patch on my chest and feed the doctor's office real-time data on my heart rhythm. I simply had to carry it around for two weeks.

Done.

I was as pumped as my heart.

When I got home, I relished my blessings. I was on the up with my health. I had my family. My business. My swanky new cardiac monitor.

It was also a lovely August day, eighty degrees, no humidity.

Perfection.

My dog Moxie and I started a lap around the yard. My type-A interests were in taking stock of the blades of grass. Moxie's interest was more focused on the sticks she could find in the yard to take back to the driveway while watching me work.

I tackled the first garden with no issue. Just had to turn the dirt over and witness the transformation.

The second garden looked a little trickier, but nothing I couldn't handle. There was a massive broadleaf weed taking up the whole left side of the garden, but that was about it. I squatted down to rip this whole thing out, from roots to leaf. I pulled.

And I felt something.

I felt something sharp.

Something painful.

And I felt it again.

I panicked, thinking that the wiring on my new monitor or phone was somehow short-circuiting and electrocuting me.

The sharp pain again.

Believe it or not, it was *not* my heart this time. I hadn't overstrained. I hadn't torn anything.

I had . . . ripped off the top of a massive beehive.

Run.

Speed Racer himself couldn't have raced faster than me. Moxie tried and was running around like crazy wondering what the hell was happening. Was it a game? Was I crazy? Was I in danger?

Definitely some danger.

The bees were in my clothes.

With no time to spare, I stripped down completely, with only my boxers to hold onto the last vestiges of dignity in this situation.

There I stood, screaming with a force that could wake the dead and swinging at anything that crossed my peripheral.

I was covered in welts, my garden was now even worse for wear than when I began, and the bees had not left.

After a quick phone call to Lisa from the inside phone to let her know what happened, I stood my six-foot-six frame up tall and grabbed a broom. These stingers were going down.

And then I could go to urgent care.

Moxie!

She had not followed me inside and was still out there with the beasts. I found her standing over my ravaged pile of clothes. I used the broom handle to carefully push around the pile when more bees flew out.

Not on my watch!

I took to the pile of clothes like it was my sole mission in life. There would be no survivors. My clothes were the innocent victim of this mission, and they finally looked as bad as my garden beds.

Still in my underwear, I started to settle down and assess my body once more.

The welts were getting bigger and . . . *oh shit*, I have a heart monitor on my chest.

The phone!

My mind was all over the place.

Confirming there were no more bees hiding in the pile of clothes, I slowly peeled them off the ground.

And there it was.

The brand-new, nine-hundred-dollar piece of innovative technology that I was lucky to try.

Oh, shit all over again.

By the time Lisa made it home, I threw on some fresh clothes to head with her to urgent care. When it was all said and done, I had been stung fifteen times. I survived.

The phone . . . did not.

The first voyage of this new device did not go well, but the office understood. I may have slightly fudged the story to say I slipped down the hill while being stung. But, either way, and pleasantly surprised, I did not have an AFib event at all. Ultimately, I got a new phone, and it confirmed that my heart was doing what it should and how it should.

I was floating high like a butterfly. But man. It sure stung like a bee.

I was starting to let my guard down now that maybe this was all *finally* behind me.

I was taking everything easy but was focused. I started reintegrating workouts into my routine. If this was my fresh chance at a healthy life, I didn't want to take it for granted.

Leading up to the radiofrequency ablation and even the cardioversion, my friends in health care told me that my cognitive abilities would improve greatly once my heart started beating regularly again.

Nice. Finally, a silver lining to all of this.

I didn't notice a particular uptake in brain power, but I did notice an uptick in headaches.

Not sharp, painful headaches, but long-lasting, mild headaches that no analgesic could touch. My father had a history of ministrokes, and strokes are the number one risk factor of atrial fibrillation.

I didn't want to panic unless I had to. My cardiologist convinced me there was no need for such thoughts. He told me that this was most likely the blood vessels in my brain *finally* opening as my persistent atrial fibrillation had decreased my brain blood flow and whole brain perfusion.

Damn. Again, I learned something new. It continued to shock me how involved I was in the medical world, yet so far removed from my own condition.

Now that my blood was circulating at a full tilt, there wasn't anything that could slow us down.

Year five for Alkemy was well on its way.

The signs were pointing to the fact that we were going to beat the odds. And this time, you didn't have to squint to see them.

Those numbers ran through my mind all the time: 20 percent of all new small businesses fail within the first two years; 45 percent of businesses fail within the first five years.

There was no time to worry about the next statistic. I may not have been beating the odds with my heart, but we were beating the odds in business at this point. As much as there had been some rocky moments, I never kept my eyes off the lighthouse in the distance. There was a reason for all of it. I *knew* it would work.

I had to make it work.

And I was.

The first order of business was to "exorcise" all the brilliant ideas out of my head. Let other people in on the genius for a change.

At times, it felt like the success of the company nearly cost me my life. But in a lot of ways, the success of the company kept me alive.

Or at least *feeling* alive.

Where my physical heart had failed, my metaphoric heart beat in appreciation for everything Alkemy was achieving.

But for me, it was more about the holistic accomplishment of it all.

It was years of my life all channeled into one successful ride.

It was the sacrifices.

Heart health.

Mental health.

Relationship health.

The *Kaveney Work Ethic*.

Except . . . I wasn't ALONE! anymore. I had people. Plural. Who were all in it for the long haul.

We were prepared for the "what's next," and it was going to be fun.

CHAPTER 20

Broken Heart, Broken Mind

My physical heart was mending just in time for it to break. My father died on January 3, 2017.

For years, his health had been in decline. The first reaction might be to blame his liver after years of alcoholism. But it wasn't his liver.

It was his mind.

His mind began to betray him in the preliminary stages of vascular dementia.

My mom was always the talker, and my dad was a man of few spoken words. But boy, could he write. He could always capture the essence of his feelings with pen and paper. My dad's dementia was more pronounced than my mom's (yes, they both developed dementia), and he unfortunately dealt with aphasia too.

The man, who used few spoken words to begin with, had to deal with the inability to comprehend or formulate language at all. When he would want to tell me he loved me, it would come out, "I like you."

As his dementia worsened, his written word would cease, and we could only share in rare moments of verbal communication.

In the summer of 2016, I rushed home to Erie because my dad was admitted to the hospital. He had become unresponsive and wasn't eating.

He was discharged to a long-term care facility, where I rode with him in the ambulance and spent the first night with him.

I never wanted *him* to be ALONE! Not as a kid, not as an adult. I could not stand the idea of leaving him alone in a foreign place. He struggled all night long breathing, and I kept praying that this was not the end.

He was not going down on my watch.

His breathing was laborious. His lips were chapped and covered with dried saliva. I cleaned his face and dabbed wet sponges on his lips and tongue to comfort him. He was out of it, but this was the only thing I could do. I felt pretty helpless, but . . .

We made it through the night.

Over the next few days, he became more acclimated to his new surroundings. I hated leaving him there, even when he was settled.

Knowing he didn't have a lot of time left, I came home to Erie more frequently to get as much time with him as possible.

He was born on December 14, and I was determined to get home and throw him a birthday party with my family. At this point, my dad was barely eating, but we knew what he would enjoy. He had an endless sweet tooth, so he would get cake, and we would toast his life with a beer.

I arrived in Erie on the thirteenth to celebrate on the fourteenth.

But, in typical fashion, Erie's unpredictable winter weather would wreak havoc on my plans.

An intense blizzard was forming and going to hit the evening of the four-teenth. If I stayed, I would be stuck for a number of days, and I needed to get home for Christmas with my boys.

Prior to catching my flight before the party, I went to spend the morning with my dad. Regardless of his inability to communicate, just being present with each other was special.

"Morning, Dad. Happy Birthday! How was your night?"

No response.

Not surprising, as he hadn't been able to communicate vocally with me in years.

When I arrived, I found him sitting in a chair outside of his room playing with some textured fabric.

I noticed he had not been shaved in a while and it looked like his face could use a wash. His face was sunken in, and I was afraid to cut him with the razor, so I left the shaving to the professionals and just washed his face. I soaked a hand towel in hot water to give him a steam wash without burning his tender skin. He laid his head back on the chair as I placed the towel over his face, and he let me clean him up, addressing his chapped lips and dried saliva.

As I was finishing and pulling away the cloth from his face, he looked me right in the eyes.

"Thank you!"

Wow.

It was his birthday, and I got the gift of hearing him speak. Those were the last words he would ever say to me.

A few weeks later, I would be back by his bedside, caring for him as his last breath approached.

Several of my siblings and I stayed with him throughout the night, and the others arrived in the morning. He was still holding strong. I am not sure why, but I was overcome with the urge to leave his side and take a shower at my brother's house nearby. I did not get more than half a block away when my cell phone rang, and my sister told me he had passed.

I missed the peaceful transition to his new afterlife.

Why did I leave? What on earth could have compelled me so strongly to walk away from his bedside at *that* moment?

My sister said he didn't want his baby to see him go. It must have been his spirit urging me out the door.

F*ck dementia.

He would finally rest from the battles he fought in his mind. Whatever demons he struggled with from his childhood were now laid to rest.

We all spent time with his body after he died, but I stayed until the undertaker arrived.

I brought him into this place; I was going to escort him out.

We shared a name; we shared a bond.

CHAPTER 21

Meet My "Maker"

M y heart broke a second time in 2017 when my two sons donned Patriots jerseys for the Super Bowl.

Technically, I missed the *actual* betrayal because I was in Vegas for the Super Bowl for a client launch meeting, but when the Patriots won, I called them in the morning to let them rub it in my face.

Thump.

Oh no.

Even though I was sitting while on the phone, I started to feel out of breath. I didn't want to mention anything, but when my heart sprang to erratic, I told the boys to put their mother on the phone and shared what was happening.

I told her that I was back in AFib.

No.

"Are you dehydrated? Did you party hard last night?"

Yes. It wasn't intended, but then it never was.

"Get some breakfast and hydrate."

I went down to meet Joan. She could sense that something wasn't right. My breathing was . . . aggressive.

Thankfully, our presentations were not until the following morning, but we had some prep work to do. The day was not going to be as we planned. I held out for a few more hours to see if I would snap back into rhythm.

No such luck. I felt like I was going to pass out. I told Joan to get an Uber. We needed to head to the hospital.

Immediately.

One benefit of being a cardiac patient is that you pretty much get to jump the line and get in quickly. The problem that day was, well, we were in Vegas. The day after the Super Bowl. The hospital was . . . a little chaotic.

They led us into a quieter, private room. Grateful for the space away from the chaos that was happening outside, I tried to make a phone call to let Lisa know what was going on, but she didn't pick up. I had no cell service.

Joan was a bit nervous about what was happening to me. They had put us into a padded, lead-plated room. No wonder we couldn't call anyone.

In came the doctor and nurses, full speed ahead.

They wasted no time in hooking me up to the EKG, and they immediately saw what was going on in my chest.

Resting heart rate of about 150 with periodic eruptions of 170.

They administered a quick IV of my go-to favorite drug, diltiazem.

They asked the standard questions.

"Were you drinking last night?"

"Yep."

"Alcohol is a known trigger for atrial fibrillation."

"I know, but I thought I was beyond this given the ablation and cardioversion."

Clearly not.

"Cocaine? You are pretty young to have this aggressive of a situation."

"Nope."

After an hour, there was still no reprieve. Hour after hour and still no change to my heart. We finally left after seven and a half hours.

Naturally, I blamed the Patriots for my cardiac relapse.

The easiest way to make God laugh? Tell Him your plans.

After seven months of feeling great and thinking it was behind me, my journey with AFib continued. Thankfully, it was only paroxysmal again.

If I didn't know my body well enough by now, I definitely would.

I knew exactly what would impact me.

I would play this game and get my routine checkups as needed. Additional options were offered, but living with paroxysmal AFib was manageable until proven otherwise.

On June 28, 2017, we celebrated Alkemy's fifth birthday.

We beat the statistics.

We cleared our revenue expectations two years in a row.

We had full-time employees all over the country.

We had momentum.

The next twelve months were a blur. We were still growing. Taking on more projects. Turning larger profits. Building new platforms.

Thump.

We kept track of accounts receivable and accounts payable and built bonus-driven incentives for our employees.

Thump.

By mid-2018, we had already beat our numbers of the previous full year. We kept things manageably chaotic.

Thump.

My heart, in the midst of it all, was not to be ignored.

A few years back, I had started an end-of-summer block party on the Friday of Labor Day weekend. It had started small with just our ten neighbors, but then, like all great things, it grew in demand.

This year was no different. It was the party of the year. We would fill up our cul-de-sac with the neighbors' lawn furniture and tents to create street living rooms. We would rent a wood-fired pizza truck, have live music, and then I would do what I like best, blow up fireworks to cap off the event. The neighbors would pitch in, and we would charge a donation to all of our guests and that money would benefit a food bank.

It was a beautiful night.

I was standing around one of the fire pits talking with our friend Nancy, feeling great, sipping on a beer, and catching up.

Midway through the conversation, Nancy asked, "How's the ticker Jimbo?"

Thump.

I can't say that by Nancy asking that question, a new AFib trigger had been established. But within five minutes of her asking that question, when I did not feel bad prior, I literally began to collapse onto her.

"Jimbo, you screwing around?"

What seemed like an eternity was only a few seconds.

Thankfully, I did not completely collapse on her. My heart kicked right back in, and I stood up tall again.

My AFib wanted to remind me who was in control.

Sneaky bastard.

Whether poor Nancy was the trigger or not, something changed that night.

Over the next few months, my AFib progressively got worse.

It's a miracle I made it through the fall.

But things only got worse for me. And for Nancy.

It was time to celebrate Halloween. Our friends, Kami and Steve, hosted a massive party every year.

I hadn't really seen Nancy since the Labor Day party. I really, truly did not blame her. I was just too busy for my own good sometimes.

Pleasantries were exchanged, and she sheepishly laughed about our last party experience.

"That's not going to happen again tonight, Jimbo, is it?"

Thump.

No, Nancy. I felt good.

Thump.

This time, it wasn't minutes.

Thump.

It was seconds.

I collapsed on Nancy. Again.

She thought I was messing with her. Again.

Unfortunately not.

I knew I needed to make a call to Dr. Philip. But before I could make the call on Monday, he called me first to check in. Coincidence, universe aligned, God watching and intervening—pick your rationale for the timing. Mine was the latter.

I let him know that it seemed the intensity of the AFib was picking up. I scheduled a follow-up appointment with him, where he prescribed a glue-on adhesive heart monitor.

I was to wear it for two weeks over the Thanksgiving holiday. I would keep it quiet with my family, but they would ask questions, and some would see what I was experiencing. Holding onto chairs and countertops, unable to raise my head, and barely maintaining the strength in my legs.

It was a nightmare I couldn't seem to wake up from.

We rolled into December relatively unscathed. My favorite holiday, Thanksgiving, was over. It was time to ramp up for Christmas.

As someone who feared the great ALONE!, our holiday season was usually packed with parties and hosting and caroling and family time. It was the best.

It was also exhausting for someone who could barely function at the most inopportune times.

On December 11, I headed to the hospital to visit Dr. Philip. I woke up feeling great with my holiday spirit in tow. It was the season of comfort and joy and *hope*. I was hopeful that my heart would get back to doing what it did best: guiding me in my dreams, not haunting my every waking moment.

Dr. Philip didn't think so.

When he came into the room, his face was ashen. Frazzled.

For a brief moment, I was worried about *his* heart.

And then he dropped the bomb.

"Mr. Kaveney, this is not good. What I think is going on . . . I have reviewed your results from your cardiac monitor from the two weeks over Thanksgiving. I am now diagnosing you with tachy-brady syndrome."

Shit.

He quickly explained what I had been feeling for all of those months.

"Your heart was going into an elevated rate, caused by your atrial fibrillation, and, well, because you were never really paroxysmal, your rate just lowered to a threshold that would have made you think it was not that high, but it was. From that extended period of time in AFib, your heart would grow tired and stop, and that is the brady. From your two weeks on the monitor, we recorded that your heart stopped thirty-two times, ranging between three and six seconds, and that is why you were feeling like you were going down.

Well, because you were. The two weeks of stopping was way too much to begin with, but what has happened since August is incredible. Your risk for loss of consciousness, which you experienced greatly, was evident, but there is a considerably increased risk for stroke. Consider yourself lucky, or as I see it, blessed."

Shit!

"We need to put a pacemaker in you immediately."

Shit!!!

I was not expecting any of this. This had to be a sick December Fools' joke. Those existed, right? Dr. Philip could secretly be a huge jokester. Any minute now, he would tell me he was kidding, hand me a candy cane, and send me on my jolly, merry way.

A man can dream, can't he? Especially when dreams were better than the nightmare that seemed to be my heart health.

I was overcome with chaos, and I broke down in tears at the cruel reality of my situation.

This was supposed to be a good week. It was also my dad's birthday week, and it was two years since his passing, and I was still emotional.

I missed him.

Dr. Philip was still in the room with me, but I felt all ALONE!

I jumped on the phone to call Lisa. I could barely contain myself long enough to share the news.

"Jimmy, what's up?"

Sniffles.

"Jim, what's wrong?"

Sniffles.

"Jimmy, I can barely hear you."

Lisa.

Between sniffles, she was only able to catch a few words, so Dr. Philip intervened and explained that I needed a pacemaker. *Immediately.* He would do the procedure the next morning. We were out of options.

What a difference a few hours can make in a day.

Dr. Philip explained the procedure, the risks, the recovery expectations. It was a very safe procedure with a low-risk rate for complications. The biggest concern was for the pacemaker to lose its ability to control the heartbeat, which is, you know, the whole point of a pacemaker.

With my heart stopping so many times for up to six seconds each time, I needed the electrical impulses of the pacemaker to jolt me back into rhythm.

Needed.

What an understatement.

Dr. Philip assured us that Christmas did not have to be canceled and that a bit of merriment was probably as good for the soul as the pacemaker was for the heart.

With the procedure scheduled for the next morning, I had two options: stay the night in the hospital or head home and come back before dawn.

The risk of getting back on the road was high. Dr. Philip did not advise it as my doctor, but since he was not a traffic officer, he could not stop me from getting behind the wheel. I had survived driving down the highway, keeping myself awake and alive to this point. What was one more drive? I had to see my kids.

I explained to them what was happening and what they could expect. I would be like Iron Man. I would have a permanent machine in my chest, helping my heart to beat. They were all on board with whatever Dad needed to make him stronger.

My heart beat a little *extra* from their love. It was the only kind of extra heartbeat I wished to have.

The procedure went smoothly.

I didn't love finding myself back on the cold steel of the operating table once again, this time right before Christmas. But I was trying to play it as cool as the table. I was good. I had everything under control.

I had to make it work.

Even though I had no real idea of what was happening to me.

Since the pacemaker would be going in just under the skin, they did not need to fully anesthetize me. They put an opaque shield over the left side of my face since the pacemaker was going into the left upper chest.

The doctor peeked around the shield to tell me he was about to begin. If I could have made a thumbs-up at the moment, I would have.

He was going to talk to me as the procedure started to ease my nerves and keep me distracted from my skin being sliced open.

The good doctor asked if I could feel the pressure of the instrument on my chest.

Nope.

Unfortunately, I could *feel* my skin being sliced open. The actual, literal slice of the knife. And I told the doctor just that.

There was some additional pressure to check and some panic.

"Shit, turn it up."

Those were the last words I heard from the doctor before waking up in recovery.

My eyelids were heavy with exhaustion after the procedure, but there was one picture I could clearly make out.

Lisa.

Sitting by my bedside, working on a project that was due at the end of the year. While I was operated on, Lisa was there to ensure that the operations of the business would not fail. She couldn't be the one in the operating room fixing my heart for me, so she did what she does best and focused on the work half of my heart, leaving the physiological stuff to the experts.

I was on the road to recovery. Our annual Christmas party went on without a hitch, but it wiped me out. My heart was weak, but steady. It was also very full of the beauty of the holiday spirit of my friends and family. We were ready to hunker down for the week.

We were going to take this time to relax. We needed it.

My Norman Rockwell painting.
The doors of the ambulance closed on the frightened faces of my boys.
I could not believe the movie night with my family was ruined in seconds.
I had been fine.
I had a pacemaker!
I had no idea I would be this close to death so close to Christmas.

The paramedic in the ambulance was working to calm me down, but to no avail. My heart rate was still sitting higher than 200 beats per minute.

Somehow, he was able to get an IV in my arm as we were speeding and bouncing out of my neighborhood. This guy was skilled. I had no idea what was being pushed into my veins, but it seemed to be working.

My heart was still out of control, but the chaos in my mind subsided.

I was becoming accustomed to the ambulance atmosphere.

My body was trembling from the cold and state of shock I was in when they wheeled me into the emergency room. They confirmed that they were starting an IV of diltiazem to try to control the severe cardiac arrhythmia and would be watching my EKG for the correction to take place.

As my room became a revolving door, every new provider was amazed at how my heart was *still* pushing against the drug's effects.

I just loved being a wonderous freakshow of a patient.

Just when it seemed I had the entire hospital staff working on me, the revolving door stopped, and we were told that it was a traumatic night. Their attention had to shift to something worse. While I wasn't exactly in a good situation myself, I knew someone else could be in a more precarious place.

Apparently, my heart and mind chose the right time to attack me that night. Fifteen minutes after the paramedics arrived at my house, a five-car pileup crashed one mile from my house on the main road running through town. The ambulance would have struggled to get to my house, and it may have been too late.

Those people, in much worse shape, were now being taken care of in the same emergency room as me. The quiet beeping of my cardiac monitors was overwhelmed by noises that sounded like a replay of the actual accident. I wanted to cry.

From gratitude that it wasn't me.

Anger that it was also me.

Exhaustion of *why me*, again.

I got a quick visit from my nurse and was told to count my blessings and settle in, as it was going to be a long night. They would keep tabs on me from their monitors at the nurse's station.

I wasn't exactly better, but I was finally more stable than others in the ER. I was no longer the priority.

Four hours after this all started, my heart was still running at 130–140 beats per minute. The diltiazem was taking much longer than expected. Drained, I passed out under the weight of the warm blankets.

What seemed like seconds passed. I woke up hours later and found my wife sleeping in chairs that could have come from an ancient bingo hall. She somehow managed to keep it all straight and pulled together even though I threw a curveball at her days before Christmas.

Again.

My heart issues for me were no longer anomalies—they had become commonplace. Common or not, I was spent, and I could see this journey was beating her up too.

Morning came, and the hectic noises of the emergency room were replaced with the hushing sounds typically found in a library. The quiet was intermittently disturbed by my heart monitor telling me what I already knew.

I finally reached a reasonable resting heart rate of 80 beats per minute.

A Christmas miracle.

I was transferred up to the cardiac floor for observation and consultation with a pulse monitor. Luckily, our family friend was a cardiac nurse practitioner at the hospital and could pull together the right team to assess the situation. They dealt with arrhythmias all the time but were surprised by how long it took for the high-dosed IV diltiazem to work. Having looked at the full events of the week prior and my extended history, they knew my heart would stay in rhythm (hip, hip, hooray), but they wanted to make sure it didn't get out of control.

It seemed a little too late for that.

It was fitting that the darkest day of my life coincided with the shortest, darkest day of the year.

Winter arrived, and each day would grow longer and brighter. Knowing there was more ahead of me, I knew I wouldn't and couldn't do it ALONE!

No matter how much I suppressed my fears and projected a position of strength, it was going to be my faith, my wife, and my kids that would carry me through this. They were the light in my world. The star on top of my tree.

CHAPTER 22

Let's Go!

The thing that most people forget about Iron Man is that he had multiple versions of machinery through the Marvel Cinematic Universe to keep him alive. He had to constantly update the hardware that kept his heart from stopping.

Stopping wasn't exactly my problem because of the surge of electricity from the pacemaker.

In fact, as long as I kept breathing, my heart would go on forever if we let it.

The problem was . . . it went too fast too often.

Like a wild stallion in a never-ending race against an invisible enemy.

When my heart went low, the pacemaker went high.

But then my heart saw its height and raised it higher.

My doctor started me on a new medicine in addition to my go-to favorite, diltiazem. They put me on flecainide (used to prevent life-threatening irregular heartbeats by slowing those electrical signals) to help slow the nerve impulses.

As luck would have it, a full dose set me back into atrial flutter.

Since the medicinal treatment was not working, they were going to pull me off that drug and try sotalol (yes, *another* beta-blocker) to help control the flutter. Dr. Philip was getting concerned and thought that if sotalol didn't work, they would pursue ablation in an expedited manner in the next few weeks. But he was hoping it was going to work. So, I went back to the hospital for sotalol to make sure I did not have an adverse event with it and another shot at cardioversion to address the flutter.

The days would slug along, but not my heart. The rhythm was still out of whack.

We tried cardioversion.

Again.

I had to be in the hospital to ensure that the drug could slowly be administered to obtain a steady-state concentration in my body and monitor my heart for any major changes in the heart rhythm beyond what was already happening.

No sense in pouring gas on the fire.

This took a few days. After a few days, the drug did not have any additional effects on my heart, which was great, but it did not have an immediate effect on the standing rhythm problem either.

There was a slight chance that they could get me in that day for an immediate cardiac ablation procedure.

Yay.

After a few hours of trying to work around the schedule, they could not make it work. Before they released me, they were going to try to cardiovert me. So, they wheeled me in and got me prepped.

They shaved my chest and prepped it for the paddles and jolt. After a few minutes of discussion, the anesthesia worked, and I was out.

It was . . . not as fun as last time.

Coming out of anesthesia, I revisited my "White boys *can* jump" material on this crowd.

In a less-than-comical tone, my doctor told me that I did have some good jumps, but the process failed.

"Take a look at your chest, Mr. Kaveney."

Oh. Shit.

Where the paddles had been placed now showed scorched skin with burn marks. There were three attempts to convert my heart, but my heart . . .

My heart was unwilling to budge.

I knew it was a stubborn mule when guiding my career choices, but *damn.*

I was shocked to hear it was just as stubborn medically.

They slathered some ointment on my chest burns and told me they'd put me on the calendar for another ablation to hopefully (and quickly) get this all fixed up.

I felt like Humpty Dumpty.

All the doctor's medicine and all the doctor's men couldn't put Jim Kaveney's heart together again.

My second ablation was scheduled for March 18.

I was pretty much working at half-pace for the first quarter of this new year. Continuing to feel the responsibility of our employees, I had to keep pushing forward. But thankfully, the team was in its own groove, doing things without me and growing rapidly. I wasn't quite sure how I felt about not being *needed.* Lisa was basically running everything by this point, and I knew the goal was to create a lean, mean, well-oiled machine that could run without me. But it felt a little weird since I wasn't exactly a well-oiled machine myself.

My second ablation was, thankfully, not as long as the grueling nine hours of the first. Coming out of anesthesia, the first sight I saw was Dr. Philip.

He had a big smile on his face.

That had to be a good sign. No one smiles like that when they have bad news.

"Mr. Kaveney, we are pretty damn confident we got it all. There was a small pin prick that was not completely ablated during the last ablation. Unfortunately, your heart was able to rewire itself after all of the issues you have been having for the last few years. But we sealed it up now and heavily tested your heart for any signs of relapse. We even were able to push an area of your cardiac tissue to get over 300 bpm for a short time! It was one of the highest rates we were ever able to capture in a controlled environment."

Fascinating.

"What do I win? A toaster?" I asked.

It was no crystal serving bowl, but I figured he'd appreciate my longing for appliances.

"Mr. Kaveney, with this ablation and your pacemaker, you will probably outlive us all—you have an unlimited heart."

Just like that, I was officially fixed, and the first quarter was done. Humpty Dumpty, it turns out, *could* be put back together again.

I would still be on a moratorium from doing anything overly active to prevent tearing. But, once it did happen, I should be aware of the tearing of the scar tissue around my pacemaker. I would like to say it was a monumental moment when I tore the tissue, but unfortunately, it was just an errant drive on the golf course.

My life settled in with a little bump on my chest to remind me of days gone by.

I was Iron Man.

Hear me roar.

I heard from someone that in life, things are not happening to you; they are happening *for* you.

Depending on the situation, this could come across as extreme toxic positivity or be a motivator to use the life events that you experience for the betterment of the world around you.

I was under the assumption that my bad cardiac days were behind me.

I wanted to take everything I had learned and get involved in making a difference in my community.

I knew how bad I had it. Sometimes I had the wherewithal to look for an automated external defibrillator (AED), but most of the time I didn't, and, quite frankly, I had never been trained how to use one.

They are exceptionally easy, by the way.

The instructions are included, and lives can be, and have been, saved. Being an athlete, I started thinking that the best way to have a long-lasting impact would be to get to the kids that play sports and teach them CPR and how to use an AED.

And so, I started another initiative with our local high school to teach them how to do Hands-Only CPR, with the tagline "Athletes Saving Athletes."

With coordination with the local American Heart Association office, a local cardiologist, school nurse, volunteer EMT, and many others, Alkemy Partners gathered over two hundred athletes on the football field to walk each of the teams through the process (which is now the preferred method until the professionals arrive).

The program was a huge success.

And a very hot day.

At 100 degrees, it was a good thing we were teaching these kids how to resuscitate.

Given my background in training, I also knew that this could not be a one-and-done event, or it would be a complete waste of time. We needed to reinforce these skills on a regular basis. We scheduled the program at the beginning of each athletic season: fall, winter, and spring.

By the middle of 2019, the Alkemy Partners trend line for the year was on a great upward slope.

Lisa was pretty much fully running all of the operations of the ship.

The ship was now massive.

The ship held many, many crew members.

The ship was steered by the *Kaveney Work Ethic* and my vision for direction, innovation, and development.

The ship was rumored to be cruising the sweet spot of potential acquisition.

As captain of the ship, I was definitely interested in this prospect of a sunny horizon in our future.

Not that I didn't love every single thing that we had built over the years. Because I did.

But if my cardiac concerns showed me anything, it was that the bigger the safety net, the better. And acquisition would provide that safety net for my family and my company.

We had embarked on an incredibly big project with a large global organization worth billions. They were predominantly an advertising agency and needed training help.

Over the summer, we got a chance to meet with the chief business development/acquisition officer. At first, I could not figure out what he wanted with a small company like ours. But, as time went on, it made sense.

We were good.

We were *very* good.

We were innovative.

We were family-run with a loyal and dedicated team.

We had created something out of nothing and knew how to sell it.

We . . .

We had charted for two years in a row on the Inc. 5000 list as one of the top growing privately held companies of 2019 and 2020.

This was huge.

Game-changing.

I had to make it work, and damn it, we did.

I was eager to get us secured in an acquisition, but I quickly learned it was not a process to be rushed. We had several meetings with some interested parties, but either we were too small for them or too big for them or it just didn't feel *right*.

I was eager, but I wasn't stupid.

These people had become my family over the years. They supported the company; they supported my inability to be present when my health took a turn. I wasn't going to just sell them off to the first buyer in hopes that it would all work out. That wasn't me. I had seen it happen too many times, and my heart always told me to run.

My heart had a lot to say these days, but the one consistency was that these people and our mission mattered.

I knew that when the *right* chance came at the *right* time, I wouldn't have to hope for the best.

It would just be the best.

CHAPTER 23

The "Vid"

J anuary 2020. A new decade. A year that we all thought was going to be the *best year ever.*

No more famous last words than those.

By mid-January, we were on the hot trail of a potential buyer. A global company.

We were now familiar with the lingo and realities of acquisition. This opportunity felt different. They liked what we had built, saw what we built for their company already, and loved our culture.

They wanted to pick us up and just plop us right down into the organization they were building.

Alkemy Partners was well accustomed by this time to suitors, so I wasn't tempted by the flattery. We had confidence in who we were and what we were building.

Alkemy Partners was not a struggling damsel looking for a savior.

We were looking for an opportunity to supersize our reach and abilities without having to invest a ton of money.

Personally, I was also looking to take care of all our employees that had joined us for the ride.

And given the risk that Lisa and I took, yeah, I wanted to protect my family too.

The meeting went really well, and we continued to talk for the next few weeks. It was getting real.

And fast.

The company was clicking on all fronts. We had more than enough business to keep us alive for the six-month window we gauged the success of our business in. But we were not coasting either.

Even though the conversation with this company moved forward, I was still seeking to build relationships and partnerships in case this whole thing blew up.

I was no stranger to the rugs being pulled out from under opportunity.

No stranger to Lucy ripping the football away from Charlie Brown.

No stranger to a never-ending field of dangled carrots.

I was looking to bring in other forms of revenue without me always having to be on the road, knocking on doors.

Our reputation was building, and there had to be more efficient ways of building the business.

January flew by and February with it. But not before an offer was put on the table for acquisition.

A *real* offer.

But we were worth more than the first pass. So, as any businessperson should do, we hunkered down and came back with a solid counteroffer a few days later. All my time was focused on selling the business and still growing it just in case something surprising came knocking. And knock it did.

Surprise #1: My mom's health was taking a turn for the worse. Her dementia had only worsened after my dad's death. She most likely only had a few days left to live.

I would fly into Erie on Monday, March 2, to be with my eight siblings and surround my mom as she made her way to Dad in Heaven.

I often referred to her as a tough ole Irish broad. She defended her family, worked for her family, so that we could have a great life. She always loved being surrounded by every one of us. I think she could feel our presence and held on and fought the entire week just to make the time together last longer.

She held out for almost five days, and she died early in the morning on Friday, March 6.

Or, as my brother Mike framed it, she died on 3/6, for her three girls and six boys.

She always did put her family first.

I was thankfully able to be by my mother's side when she died, and we held the funeral services the following week. I flew home to New Hampshire and gathered Lisa and the kids.

We would hold a standard Irish viewing, Mass, and wake with a lot of people. When you have this many kids, you know a lot of people.

While I hated to see my mom go, I was happy that she passed and left this world in the manner that she did. She died with us all around her, like everyone should have been able too.

Surprise #2: Global pandemic.

Within twenty-four hours of laying my mother to rest, the world shut its doors.

The big-ticket events led the way with the NBA and NHL suspending their seasons.

Schools shut down for fifteen days to slow the curve of this rapidly spreading disease.

No one predicted that fifteen days would turn into fifteen months.

There were horror stories of the nursing homes leading to significant deaths in the most vulnerable people in our country. People were dying, but there would be no funerals. Nobody could get in to see their loved ones. I missed my parents every day but found solace in the fact that this was not our family's reality.

Each day, the stories would pile up, like the numbers of people dying. We had to create bubbles within families to socialize with some friends and family. We chose our group and stayed within it.

The world was, to put it lightly, f*cked.

Like most families during this time, our home life changed dramatically.

Our business, because we were in health care, was deemed *essential* and remained open.

We were a virtual company before all of this, so we had no problem with working from home. We were prepared. We continued to churn.

The pharmaceutical industry kept its salespeople home during the pandemic, some for the rest of the year. They had salespeople at home, not selling, so something had to be done.

Well, the companies turned to pumping their employees with more training materials.

We were very busy and, in some cases, couldn't keep up with the demand.

I don't think I could have been more grateful for our setup than I was in 2020.

Ironic, right?

While business was rolling in, it wasn't new business. We found that all of the business came from our current clients doing more and more to keep their people busy. No company was interested in starting with a new training company or even switching when the influx of money was questionable at best and nonexistent at worst.

The operations of Alkemy were pumping left and right.

I would find myself spending hours and hours jumping on the trampoline outside with my boys and playing games inside, keeping them active and their minds focused. I would be the only one who went to the grocery store to keep the pantry stocked.

I was the designated leader of Team K.

Soon, remote schooling would come into play, and managing my kids and their psyches was critical. Lisa and I split duties as we were also keeping the business moving along. The first few days were OK, but the lockdowns got old real fast. Like everyone, we overplayed the Zoom meetings, Zoom happy hours, Zoom dinner dates, you name it.

Isolation was the great ALONE!, and quarantine was the perfect storm for negative thoughts.

We connected as much as we could to keep the socialization going. But nothing would, or could, replace the feeling of making true connections with handshakes, hugs, fist bumps, or just physically being in the same room as other adults.

Non-Surprise #3: The offer of acquisition was put on hold. There were two things that made investors pause.

Greed and fear.

Fear had the world at its fingertips.

Nobody had any idea how this was all going to shake out. The deal wasn't off, it was just "paused" until things became clear.

I had *finally* gotten my heart to stop pausing at the worst times possible only to now have momentum in my business paused.

It could be possible that the whole deal would be off, but that was not the decision at this point.

We understood.

Alkemy was exploding, but I also saw what was happening in pharma. If salespeople had to stay home for months and months . . .

Yeah, we *might* be able to make it through the year. Our business was growing rapidly, but like many small businesses, Lisa and I carried the burden of this thing staying afloat. Getting acquired by this company would have protected our employees, but at this point, it was moot.

$$\sim\!\!\!\!\!\wedge\!\!\!\!\sim$$

Right around the beginning of June 2020, I got *the* call.

This global company, EVERSANA, was ready to move forward with the deal.

Wow.

This was going to happen.

We would do one last bit of negotiations and verbally agree.

Almost to the date of Alkemy's June 28 birthday.

Damn, we crushed it.

We persevered.

We were going to close the sale at the end of July.

On the day of Alkemy's eighth birthday, I gathered the team together and spent an hour reflecting on how far we had come, comparing images of some of the early materials we called "good" to what we were now building. It was amazing to see how far we had grown. The Alkemy product was all grown up and strutting its stuff. We had made it through the awkward teenage years of uncertainty and become something beautiful.

Historic Perspective of the Management of the Disease State.

Innovation.

Training.

Hell. Yes.

I shared the growth of the company by personnel and revenue and thanked them for all that they did. It was the middle of the year and every single one of them, including our closest vendor partners, would get a bonus for doing so well by the middle of the year. We were very close to matching the revenue from all of 2019 by July and would surpass my original revenue goals for Alkemy Partners by miles.

I announced that we were recognized as a Health and Wellness Organization "company to watch." We would have also been ranked again by Inc. 5000 had we not been acquired.

Acquired.

Everyone at Alkemy knew the company because we had been working with them for almost a year and a half. But, as I made it through the presentation and finally shared the news that we would all be employees, a few of them virtually fell out of their chairs, tears started falling, and of course, concern, apprehension, and all things that come with change arose.

The July closing date would come and go and be pushed out to the end of August due to some additional processes, which I think was a good thing overall.

It gave our team more time to get comfortable with the integration process. The company was going to pick us up and drop us into their system. This would not be an *alliance*. I made sure everyone knew the difference. It had been years since the fateful *alliance* day, but the memories of the right way to do things still sat with me.

We as a team would continue to work as we always did and report to the same people as we always did; the only difference would be where the paycheck would come from.

$$\sim\!\!\!\bigwedge\!\!\!\sim$$

The smell of office supplies infiltrated my system once again in a life-changing way.

Stacks and stacks of paper filled the table, summarizing the small business journey of Alkemy Partners.

On August 31 at 5:00 p.m., Lisa and I signed all of the documents. She and I were both brought into the company as vice presidents. It was exhilarating to see her unfailing work over the years with Alkemy be recognized. She was one-half of the partners in every way possible.

Signatures on the forms completed, she looked at me.

"Is that it?"

No balloons.

No confetti.

No flash mob breaking out in a "Hallelujah" chorus.

No shaking hands.

No mantras to convince myself of this reality.

It was just us.

The two halves of my heart were at one. I had always known that if I listened to one half, it would always lead me to the other. My heart was unstoppable in more ways than one, and I was never going to *not* listen to it again.

But my mind . . .

My mind was looking at the acquisition signatures in front of us.

I couldn't help myself. Blame the *Kaveney Work Ethic* if you will, but I was sure I heard the faintest inner whispers of a question.

So, Jim, what's next?

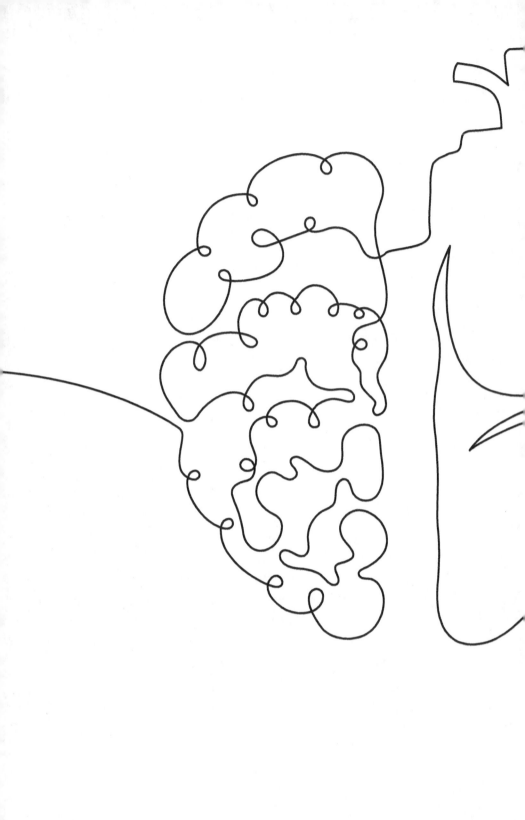

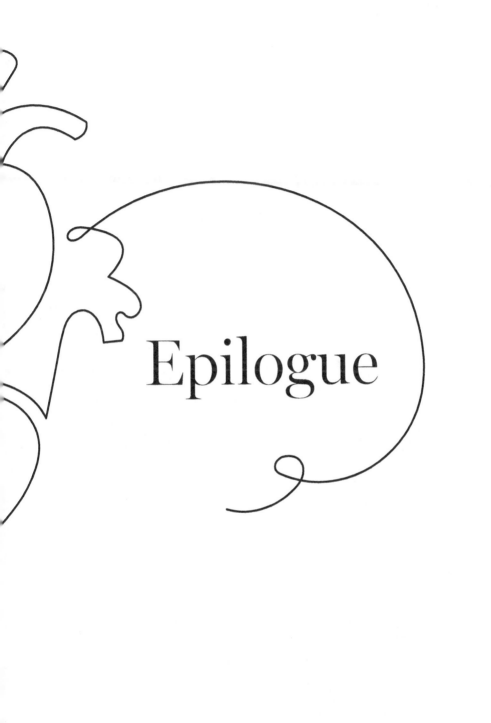

Epilogue

Epilogue

I had always known that my time at EVERSANA had an expiration date. I had signed on for three years, and when the time came, I felt I had fulfilled my mission and that it was OK to move on.

It was.

Over the course of three years, what Alkemy brought to the table for this company was unlike anything else in the industry.

Before we were acquired, I started intensely and intentionally reading up on mindset training. Just as *the book* had changed my outlook on small business leadership, other mindset and performance books had a similar effect on my outlook on training.

Yes, the HPMDS had gotten us far in building training modules and programs for companies, but I realized that if we truly, *truly* wanted to see lasting effects of product promotion, every person involved in the product (from field personnel to corporate leaders) had to shift their habits and behaviors. It was encouraging a much deeper dive into the ever-present *why* of pharmaceuticals.

And this *why* could no longer be ignored.

Pharmaceuticals as a whole is a . . . less-than-perfect industry. It's true that there is no such thing as a perfect industry, but pharma has a particularly bad rap. Most nonpharma people, when they think about pharmaceuticals, think:

Insulin prices.

Opioid crisis.

Health care expenses.

Crippling debt.

Red tape.

The list could go on and on.

As someone who has been in the industry for a very long time now, I am not blinded by the opportunities afforded to me because of my career in pharmaceuticals.

But . . .

And it's a big "but" . . .

If I walked away from pharmaceuticals because of all the bad shit, I wouldn't be able to help change what needs changing. If all the people with good intentions and high hopes removed themselves from a sticky situation, what would be left? Just stickiness.

Sometimes, Alkemy landed a company client with a dud of a product. And it was up to us to seek that product's value and build a training program around it. Some might call this *spinning the narrative*. I called it a challenge.

The drug was made for a reason, right? It was up to us to truly dig into the original instigator for that reason and help others see the value.

This is what I believed in.

Innovation.

Life-saving medicines.

Quality of life.

Longevity of life.

Helping companies bring the right product to the right people for the right reason.

And to do this, they *really* had to change their approach to sales.

We were doing a great job on building these respective skills, but what about changing people's behaviors that could help to build better habits that would build better people, better results, and drive performance?

Our *why* was always to drive performance.

We did not want to build another selling model, we wanted to build a new approach that would build skills and habits. We created a program that would do that with our mindset partners.

We eventually launched our Skillset x Mindset = Performance approach. We never wanted to slow down in innovation. We knew that it did not matter if the teams were educated at the highest level but could not perform. Skillset x Mindset would handle that. This would impact the performance of every single person, personally and professionally.

Mindset training was a bit of a slow roll out. With COVID-19 and then the acquisition, we had a lot of false starts in kicking something off the ground. But once acquisition took place and everyone settled into their roles, I really pushed for mindset initiatives.

As I said before, one of my greatest strengths is bringing together two seemingly disparate concepts into one. Here, it would be pharmaceutical sales training and mindset training.

I knew in that never-failing heart of mine that the two things could work together to create something beautiful in an industry that couldn't hurt to embrace a little more beauty.

That being said, it's not all bad. In fact, I would say that it's all *mostly* good.

Innovation.

What life sciences brings to the world on a literal global scale is innovation. New technologies. New breakthroughs in treating comorbidities. New procedures and medicine. New studies on wellness.

I believe wholeheartedly (even with my troublesome whole heart) that what comes out of the pharma world is far greater than some of the surrounding issues.

I always knew I wanted to start another company. Alkemy Partners was a dream come true, but once my heart whispered *it was time*, my head took action.

For me, Unlimited Heart Health and Wellness isn't just a cheeky play on the fact that my heart can literally not stop beating; it is an entire outlook.

A game-changer in the field of cardiac health.

I was someone who worked in the health care industry, yet I had to punch my leg to prevent myself from falling asleep at the wheel from heart issues.

I had every possible source of information at my fingertips, yet I knew next to nothing about how to care for myself.

I was breathing life into a new company while simultaneously trying to catch my own irregular breath.

I never wanted to be a statistic about men's heart health, and I don't want anyone, any person, to feel this way either.

If I had applied the same rigor of gut feeling and practical knowledge to my health as I had my career, things might have gone a little smoother. I spent years teaching myself how to *think* my way out of difficult situations.

I had my mantras.

My consistent "go get 'em" mentality every time I needed to take a deep breath before diving into yet another job search.

But I didn't . . . I couldn't . . . do the same when it came to my physical heart.

Through the business of Unlimited Heart, I want to ignite the passion of mindset training and patient/caregiver education and empowerment with the innovations of biotech and the severity of cardiac health.

My heart will never stop beating.

Not literally.

And not metaphorically for bettering the lives of anyone who needs it.

This time will be different.

I won't let my fear of being ALONE! be a hindrance to the start of this initiative. This is not going to be me opening a laptop and saying: "I am in business."

This is going to take a team; this is greater than just my heart and mind.

I believe that knowledge does not equal power. So, having knowledge about the heart and mind separately means that knowledge flatlines.

But, merging the knowledge of the heart and mind and directing it to a specific approach . . . now *that* is powerful.

Unlimited Heart is being built to be an accelerator of that power. Turning my pain into purpose. Into an entity resting firmly on the four pillars of work-life-faith-health balance. I believe, through education and empowerment of the mind and the heart, that we can build "better people" and in turn build "better AFib patients."

Join us.

Let's go far.

Let's go together.

Let's keep on . . .

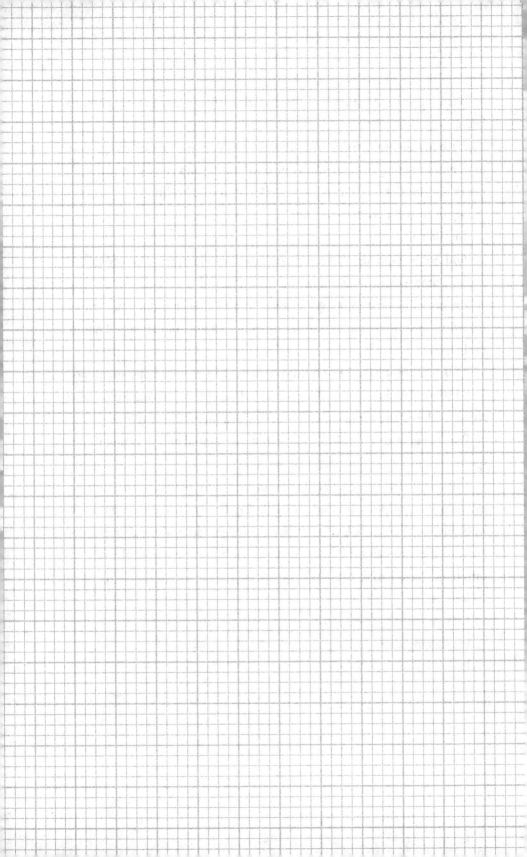

Acknowledgments

Don't write a book unless you have a purpose . . .

Shortly after my team at Alkemy Partners grew our business into one of the fastest growing private small businesses in America by *Inc.* magazine, I started receiving calls from book publishers eager to sell my *success story.*

"People need to hear about your story," they would say.

"No, they don't," I kept replying.

I could not see how our success was different than the other small businesses that struggle, persevere, and overcome hurdles to reach their goals. My story could have been copied and pasted from thousands of other successful stories out there.

What would be the purpose of that?

No purpose, no book.

Thank you, Natasha Walstra, for that mantra.

Years passed, and Team Alkemy was fully integrated into EVERSANA and grew beyond my wildest dreams. It was time to execute the all-powerful *What's next?!*

But . . . what would actually be next?

I couldn't envision a book solely centered around Alkemy's success.

But . . . I *could* envision a book centered around my entire life journey and how it got me to where I am today and where I want to go tomorrow.

Believe it or not, this actually felt a lot less daunting.

My *purpose* was finally defined: serve others.

My story of faith, family, entrepreneurship, learning and performance, atrial fibrillation diagnosis, and being one heartbeat away from meeting my maker would become the foundation of the book.

This quickly became my *What's next?!*

So, there we sat. Lisa and me, eating a quiet meal in her "happy place" in Maine. I began to share my vision for what's next, and I sketched it all out for her at the table. When I looked up to gather her reaction, there were tears rolling down her face.

"What's wrong?"

"Nothing . . . it's a beautiful vision. Go for it."

And so, with her blessing and continued support, I set off to write the book and hopefully change the world for patients with atrial fibrillation and my fellow entrepreneurs.

Success does not occur in a vacuum, and without question for me, it does not happen without *Lisa*.

So, to Lisa . . .

I could not have done any of this without you. I am not sure you knew that I was a restless soul, always looking for a greater purpose in the things I do. Which can be . . . exhausting. But without fail, there you are, by my side. My big ideas are fun and exciting, but invariably, there is so much work that comes along with them. If it wasn't for your love, leadership, and general kick-ass skills, my grand ideas would remain as nothing more than that . . . ideas.

To my Kaveney Men: Marcus and Ian . . .

While you have been my sons for 30 percent of my years, you are 100 percent of my life. This book was written for a broad audience, but it is for *you*. You were just little boys when you witnessed your father go through some rather . . . dark and tough times. But, as you grow into men, I hope you see that darkness and adversity can be overcome with faith, family, and friends. My days are the brightest now because of you. I am so excited to see where the *Kaveney Work Ethic* takes you.

To my wonderful parents . . .

You taught me about the *Kaveney Work Ethic*, or what is now known as grit. You taught me that nothing replaces honest, hard work, your family, or faith. You are no longer with us, but your life lessons live on in me, your other eight children, and your forty-plus grandchildren.

And to my sisters and brothers (JoAnne, Tommy, Jeffrey, Brian, Billy, Mike, Cathleen, and Suzanne) and your respective spouses (who I have known long enough to call you my sisters and brothers) . . .

Thank you for your constant support, guidance, and influence. Let's keep growing together for the next generation to carry on.

To Lisa's parents and sisters . . .

When we moved from Erie, you quickly filled in my need for family and have done more for us over the years than you can ever imagine.

To my chosen family, my friends . . .

My mom always said that I had a friend in every port, and I am blessed to be able to say that is true. I am a rich man to say that I have such great old *and* new friends. From grade school to high school, through college and countless hours on the water to the bountiful yields of the vineyards in New Hampshire, my cup is full and overflowing. Grateful for you all doesn't even begin to cover it.

To my team from Alkemy and EVERSANA . . .
If it wasn't for you, the ideas in my head would not come to life and the impact on the industry in which we serve would not have happened. *You* are the difference makers. But, without the believers that took a chance on all of us, our customers, clients, partners . . . none of this would exist. You are the bold ones for believing in us. There are not enough ways to say thank you.

To my beta readers: Lisa M., Amy & Cesar, Kami & Steve, and Steve B . . .
You were exposed to the raw footage. Your insights helped shape the flow, direction, and purpose of the book.

To my editing and publishing team . . .
I had no idea how beautiful a few words could become until you got a hold of them. Megan Barnes, founder of Two Tales Editing, master editor and writer, it is my storytelling behind the book, but it is *your* telling of the story that made the words come to life. I could not, and would not, have wanted to do this with anyone else.

Rohit Bhargava, Megan Wheeler, Marnie McMahon, Kameron Bryant-Sergejev, and the entire team at Ideapress Publishing . . .
Thank you for seeing *Unlimited Heart* as more than just a memoir, but as a potential opportunity to truly change people's lives. Given this is my first rodeo in book publishing, you made it seamless and easy. And to David Grillo for adding your creative genius to the book through your line drawings.

And most importantly . . .

If you are reading these words, you invested time, energy, and money into reading my story. Thank you! I hope these words help you to keep moving and fighting the fight to make a difference in your world.

Work with Jim

Everyone battles their own pain in life. Whether it is big or small, it's still *your* pain.

So, own it.

Take control of it and maintain your power over it.

If you are ready to transform your pain into a purpose, I would welcome the opportunity to work with you and help you through your journey.

If you are a cardiac patient dealing with atrial fibrillation and trying to master your lifestyle choices, and you are looking for a vehicle to help you along your journey, please reach out to me at **info@unlimitedheart.co** or find additional information at **www.UnlimitedHeart.co**.

If you are not an atrial fibrillation patient, but want to take the next steps to transforming yourself, please reach out to me at **info@unlimitedheart.co** or find additional information at **www.UnlimitedHeart.co**.

Order copies of *Unlimited Heart* for your team or organization.

Would you like to buy multiple copies of *Unlimited Heart* to share with your team or organization? Contact my team at **bulkorders@unlimitedheart.co** to learn about bulk order discounts to meet your needs.

Want to read *Unlimited Heart* as part of a book club? Want to learn how to transform your pain into a purpose? Or join our cause at Unlimited Heart? Go to **www.UnlimitedHeart.co** for more information.

Speaking and Workshops

If you enjoyed the book and are motivated by it and think it could make a difference in your life or others, I would be happy to come and collaborate with you at your next conference or event.

Standalone keynotes, educational workshops, and transformational learning journeys are how we are operationalizing our difference-making. Please contact me directly. No one should be alone in their journey.

Connect with Me

✉ : info@unlimitedheart.co

in : linkedin.com/in/jameskaveney

linkdedin.com/company/unlimited-heart-health-wellness

linkedin.com/company/unlimited-heart-book

⊙ : jimkaveney_unlimitedheart